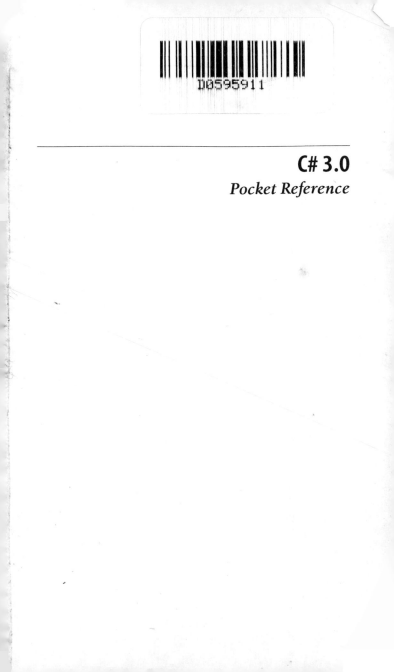

C# 3.0
Pocket Reference

SECOND EDITION

C# 3.0
Pocket Reference

Joseph Albahari and Ben Albahari

O'REILLY®

Beijing · Cambridge · Farnham · Köln · Sebastopol · Taipei · Tokyo

C# 3.0 Pocket Reference, Second Edition

by Joseph Albahari and Ben Albahari

Published by O'Reilly Media, Inc., 1005 Gravenstein Highway North, Sebastopol, CA 95472.

O'Reilly books may be purchased for educational, business, or sales promotional use. Online editions are also available for most titles (*safari.oreilly.com*). For more information, contact our corporate/institutional sales department: (800) 998-9938 or *corporate@oreilly.com*.

Editor: Laurel R.T. Ruma
Production Editor: Loranah Dimant
Proofreader: Loranah Dimant
Indexer: Angela Howard

Cover Designer: Karen Montgomery
Interior Designer: David Futato
Illustrator: Jessamyn Read

Printing History:

November 2002:	First Edition.
February 2008:	Second Edition.

ISBN: 978-0-596-51922-3
[TM]   [6/08]

Contents

C# 3.0 Pocket Reference

C# is a general-purpose, type-safe, object-oriented programming language whose goal is programmer productivity. To this
end, the language balances simplicity, expressiveness, and performance. The C# language is platform-neutral, but it was
written to work well with the Microsoft .NET Framework.
C# 3.0 targets .NET Framework 3.5.

What's New in C# 3.0

C# 3.0 features are centered on Language Integrated Query
capabilities, or LINQ for short. LINQ enables SQL-like queries to be written directly within a C# program, and checked
statically for correctness. Queries can execute either locally
or remotely; the .NET Framework provides LINQ-enabled
APIs across local collections, remote databases, and XML.

C# 3.0 features include:

- Lambda expressions
- Extension methods
- Implicitly typed local variables
- Query comprehensions
- Anonymous types
- Implicitly typed arrays
- Object initializers
- Automatic properties

- Partial methods
- Expression trees

Lambda expressions are like miniature functions created on the fly. They are a natural evolution of anonymous methods introduced in C# 2.0, and in fact, completely subsume the functionality of anonymous methods. For example:

```
Func<int,int> sqr = x => x * x;
Console.WriteLine (sqr(3));        // 9
```

The primary use case in C# is with LINQ queries, such as the following:

```
string[] names = { "Tom", "Dick", "Harry" };

// Include only names of >= 4 characters:

IEnumerable<string> filteredNames =
  Enumerable.Where (names, n => n.Length >= 4);
```

Extension methods extend an existing type with new methods, without altering the type's definition. They act as syntactic sugar, making static methods feel like instance methods. Because LINQ's query operators are implemented as extension methods, we can simplify our preceding query as follows:

```
IEnumerable<string> filteredNames =
  names.Where (n => n.Length >= 4);
```

Implicitly typed local variables let you omit the variable type in a declaration statement, allowing the compiler to infer it. Because the compiler can determine the type of filteredNames, we can further simplify our query:

```
var filteredNames = names.Where (n => n.Length == 4);
```

Query comprehension syntax provides SQL-style syntax for writing queries. Comprehension syntax can simplify certain kinds of queries substantially, as well as serving as syntactic sugar for lambda-style queries. Here's the previous example in comprehension syntax:

```
var filteredNames = from n in names
                    where n.Length >= 4
                    select n;
```

Anonymous types are simple classes created on the fly, and are commonly used in the final output of queries:

```
var query = from n in names where n.Length >= 4
            select new {
                          Name = n,
                          Length = n.Length
                       };
```

Here's a simpler example:

```
var dude = new { Name = "Bob", Age = 20 };
```

Implicitly typed arrays eliminate the need to state the array type, when constructing and initializing an array in one step:

```
var dudes = new[]
{
    new { Name = "Bob", Age = 20 },
    new { Name = "Rob", Age = 30 }
};
```

Object initializers simplify object construction by allowing properties to be set inline after the constructor call. Object initializers work with both anonymous and named types. For example:

```
Bunny b1 = new Bunny {
                        Name = "Bo",
                        LikesCarrots = true,
                     };
```

The equivalent in C# 2.0 is:

```
Bunny b2 = new Bunny( );
b2.Name = "Bo";
b2.LikesCarrots = false;
```

Automatic properties cut the work in writing properties that simply get/set a private backing field. In the following example, the compiler automatically generates a private backing field for X:

```
public class Stock
{
  public decimal X { get; set; }
}
```

Partial methods let an auto-generated partial class provide customizable hooks for manual authoring. LINQ to SQL makes use of partial methods for generated classes that map SQL tables.

Expression trees are miniature code DOMs that describe lambda expressions. The C# 3.0 compiler generates expression trees when a lambda expression is assigned to the special type Expression<TDelegate>:

```
Expression<Func<string,bool>> predicate =
  s => s.Length > 10;
```

Expression trees make it possible for LINQ queries to execute remotely (e.g., on a database server) because they can be introspected and translated at runtime (e.g., into an SQL statement).

A First C# Program

Here is a program that multiplies 12×30, and prints the result, 360, to the screen. The double-forward slash indicates that the remainder of a line is a *comment*.

```
using System;                // importing namespace

class Test                   // class declaration
{
  static void Main()         //   method declaration
  {
    int x = 12 * 30;         //     statement 1
    Console.WriteLine (x);   //     statement 2
  }                          //   end of method
}                            // end of class
```

At the heart of this program lie two *statements*. Statements in C# execute sequentially. Each statement is terminated by a semicolon:

```
int x = 12 * 30;
Console.WriteLine (x);
```

The first statement computes the *expression* 12 * 30 and stores the result in a *local variable*, named x, which is an integer type. The second statement calls the Console class's WriteLine method to print the variable x to a text window on the screen.

A *method* performs an action in a series of statements, called a *statement block*—a pair of braces containing zero or more statements. We defined a single method named Main:

```
static void Main( )
{
  ...
}
```

Writing higher-level functions that call upon lower-level functions simplifies a program. We can refactor our program with a reusable method that multiplies an integer by 12 as follows:

```
using System;

class Test
{
  static void Main( )
  {
    Console.WriteLine (FeetToInches (30));    // 360
    Console.WriteLine (FeetToInches (100));   // 1200
  }

  static int FeetToInches (int feet)
  {
    int inches = feet * 12;
    return inches;
  }
}
```

A method can receive *input* data from the caller by specifying *parameters*, and *output* data back to the caller by specifying a *return type*. We defined a method called FeetToInches that has a parameter for inputting feet, and a return type for outputting inches:

```
static int InchesToFeet (int feet) {...}
```

The *literals* 30 and 100 are the *arguments* passed to the FeetToInches method. The Main method in our example has empty parentheses because it has no parameters, and it is void because it doesn't return any value to its caller:

```
static void Main()
```

C# recognizes a method called Main as signaling the default entry point of execution. The Main method may optionally return an integer (rather than void) to return a value to the execution environment. The Main method can also optionally take an array of string arguments (that will be populated with any arguments passed to the executable). For example:

```
static int Main (string[] args) {...}
```

NOTE

An array (such as string[]) represents a fixed number of elements of a particular type (see the upcoming "Arrays," section).

Methods are one of several kinds of functions in C#. Another kind of function we used was the * *operator*, used to perform multiplication. There are also *constructors*, *properties*, *events*, *indexers*, and *finalizers*.

In our example, the two methods are grouped into a class. A *class* groups function members and data members to form an object-oriented building block. The Console class groups members that handle command-line input/output functionality, such as the WriteLine method. Our Test class groups two methods—the Main method and the FeetToInches method. A class is a kind of *type*, which we will examine later in the "Type Basics" section.

At the outermost level of a program, types are organized into *namespaces*. The using directive made the System namespace available to our application, so we could reference System.Console without the System. prefix. We

---

could define all our classes within the TestPrograms namespace, as follows:

```
using System;

namespace TestPrograms
{
  class Test  {...}
  class Test2 {...}
}
```

The .NET Framework is organized into nested namespaces. For example, this is the namespace that contains types for handling text:

```
using System.Text;
```

The using directive is there for convenience; you can also refer to a type by its fully qualified name, which is the type name prefixed with its namespace, such as System.Text. StringBuilder.

Compilation

The C# compiler compiles source code, specified as a set of files with the *.cs* extension, into an assembly. An *assembly* is the unit of packaging and deployment in .NET., and it can be either an application or a library. A normal console or Windows *application* has a Main method and is an *.exe*. A *library* is a *.dll*, and is equivalent to an *.exe* without an entry point. Its purpose is to be called upon (referenced) by an application or by other libraries. The .NET Framework is a set of libraries.

The name of the C# compiler is *csc.exe*. You can either use an IDE such as Visual Studio .NET to call csc automatically, or compile manually from the command line. To compile manually, first save a program to a file such as *MyFirstProgram.cs*, and then invoke csc (located under *<windows>/Microsoft. NET/Framework*) from the command line, as follows:

```
csc MyFirstProgram.cs
```

This produces an application named *MyFirstProgram.exe*. To produce a library (*.dll*), you'd do the following:

```
csc /target:library MyFirstProgram.cs
```

Syntax

C# syntax is based on C and C++ syntax. In this section, we describe C#'s elements of syntax, using the following program:

```
using System;

class Test
{
  static void Main()
  {
    int x = 12 * 30;
    Console.WriteLine (x);
  }
}
```

Identifiers and Keywords

Identifiers are names that programmers choose for their classes, methods, variables, and so on. These are the identifiers in our example program in the order in which they appear:

```
System    Test    Main    x    Console    WriteLine
```

An identifier must be a whole word, essentially made up of Unicode characters starting with a letter or underscore. C# identifiers are case-sensitive. By convention, arguments, local variables, and private fields should be in camel case (e.g., myVariable), and all other identifiers should be in Pascal case (e.g., MyMethod).

Keywords are names reserved by the compiler that you can't use as identifiers. These are the keywords in our example program:

```
using    class    static    void    int
```

Here is the full list of C# keywords:

abstract	enum	long	stackalloc
as	event	namespace	static
base	explicit	new	string
bool	extern	null	struct
break	false	object	switch
byte	finally	operator	this
case	fixed	out	throw
catch	float	override	true
char	for	params	try
checked	foreach	private	typeof
class	goto	protected	uint
const	if	public	ulong
continue	implicit	readonly	unchecked
decimal	in	ref	unsafe
default	int	return	unsafe
delegate	interface	sbyte	ushort
do	internal	sealed	using
double	is	short	virtual
else	lock	sizeof	void
			while

Avoiding conflicts

If you really want to use an identifier that clashes with a key word, you can qualify it with the @ prefix. For instance:

```
class class  {...}    // illegal
class @class {...}    // legal
```

The @ symbol doesn't form part of the identifier itself, so @myVariable is the same as myVariable.

Contextual keywords

Some keywords are *contextual*, meaning that they can also be used as identifiers—without an @ symbol. The following are contextual keywords:

add	get	let	set
ascending	global	on	value
by	group	orderby	var
descending	in	partial	where
equals	into	remove	yield
from	join	select	

With contextual keywords, ambiguity cannot arise within the context in which they are used.

Literals, Punctuators, and Operators

Literals are primitive pieces of data statically embedded into the program. The literals in our example program are 12 and 30.

Punctuators help demarcate the structure of the program. These are the punctuators in our example program:

```
;   {   }
```

The semicolon is used to terminate a statement and allows statements to wrap multiple lines:

```
Console.WriteLine
    (1 + 2 + 3 + 4 + 5 + 6 + 7 + 8 + 9 + 10);
```

The braces are used to group multiple statements into a statement block.

Operators transform and combine expressions. Most operators in C# are denoted with a symbol, such as the multiplication operator, *. We will discuss operators in more detail later in this book. These are the operators we used in our example program:

```
.   ()   *   =
```

The period refers to a member of something. The parentheses are used when declaring or calling a method; empty parentheses are used when the method does not accept arguments. The equals sign is used for *assignment* (the double-equals sign, ==, is used for equality comparison).

Comments

C# offers two different styles of source code documentation: single-line comments and multiline comments. A single-line comment begins with a double-forward slash and continues until the end of the line. For example:

```
int x = 3;   // comment about assigning 3 to x
```

A multiline comment begins with /* and ends with */:

```
int x = 3;   /* this is a comment that
                spans two lines */
```

Comments may embed XML documentation tags (see the upcoming "XML Documentation" section).

Type Basics

A *type* defines the blueprint for a value. A *value* is a storage location denoted by a variable or a constant. A *variable* represents a value that can change, whereas a *constant* represents an invariant. We created a local variable named x in our first program:

```
static void Main()
{
  int x = 12 * 30;
  Console.WriteLine (x);
}
```

All values in C# are *instances* of a specific type. The meaning of a value, and the set of possible values a variable can have, is determined by its type. The type of x is int.

Predefined Type Examples

Predefined types are types that are specially supported by the compiler. The int type is a predefined primitive type for representing the set of integers that fits into 32 bits of memory, from -2^{31} to $2^{31}-1$. We can perform functions such as arithmetic with instances of the int type, as follows:

```
int x = 12 * 30;
```

Another predefined C# type is the string type. The string type represents a sequence of characters, such as ".NET" or "http://oreilly.com". We can manipulate strings by calling functions on them as follows:

```
string message = "Hello world";
string upperMessage = message.ToUpper();
Console.WriteLine (upperMessage);        // HELLO WORLD

int x = 2007;
message = message + x.ToString();
Console.WriteLine (message);             // Hello world2007
```

The primitive bool type has exactly two possible values: true and false. The bool type is commonly used to conditionally branch execution flow based with an if statement. For example:

```
bool simpleVar = false;
if (simpleVar)
  Console.WriteLine ("This will not print");

int x = 5000;
bool lessThanAMile = x < 5280;
if (lessThanAMile)
  Console.WriteLine ("This will print");
```

NOTE

In C#, predefined types (also referred to as *built-in types*) are recognized with a C# keyword. The System namespace in the .NET Framework contains many important types that C# does not predefine (e.g., DateTime).

Custom Type Examples

Just as we can build complex functions from simple functions, we can build complex types from primitive types. In this example, we will define a custom type named UnitConverter—a class that serves as a blueprint for unit conversions:

```
using System;

public class UnitConverter
{
  int ratio;                          // Field

  public UnitConverter (int unitRatio) // Constructor
    { ratio = unitRatio; }

  public int Convert (int unit)       // Method
    { return unit * ratio; }
}

class Test
{
  static void Main( )
  {
    UnitConverter feetToInches = new UnitConverter(12);
    UnitConverter milesToFeet = new UnitConverter(5280);

    Console.Write (feetToInches.Convert(30));  // 360
    Console.Write (feetToInches.Convert(100)); // 1200
    Console.Write (feetToInches.Convert
                   (milesToFeet.Convert(1))); // 63360
  }
}
```

Members of a type

A type contains *data members* and *function members*. The data member of UnitConverter is the *field* called ratio. The function members of UnitConverter are the Convert method and the UnitConverter's constructor.

Symmetry of predefined types and custom types

A beautiful aspect of C# is that predefined types and custom types have few differences. The primitive int type serves as a blueprint for integers. It holds data—32 bits—and provides function members that use that data, such as ToString. Similarly, our custom UnitConverter type acts as a blueprint for unit conversions. It holds data—the ratio—and provides function members to use that data.

Constructors and instantiation

Data is created by *instantiating* a type. Primitive types can be instantiated simply by using a literal. For example, the following line instantiates two integers (12 and 30), which are used to compute a third instance, x:

```
int x = 12 * 30;
```

The new operator is needed to create a new instance of a custom type. We created and declared an instance of the UnitConverter type with this statement:

```
UnitConverter feetToInchesConverter =
   new UnitConverter(12);
```

Immediately after the new operator instantiates an object, the object's constructor is called to perform initialization. A constructor is defined like a method, except that the method name and return type are reduced to the name of the enclosing type:

```
public class UnitConverter
{
   ...
   public UnitConverter (int r)    // Constructor
     { ratio = r; }
   ...
}
```

Instance versus static members

The data members and function members that operate on the *instance* of the type are called instance members. The UnitConverter's Convert method and the int's ToString method are examples of instance members. By default, members are instance members.

Data members and function members that don't operate on the instance of the type, but rather on the type itself, must be marked as static. The Test.Main and Console.WriteLine methods are static methods. The Console class is actually a *static class*, where *all* its members are static. You never actually create instances of a Console—one console is shared across the whole application.

To contrast instance versus static members, the instance field Name pertains to an instance of a particular Panda, whereas Population pertains to the set of all Panda instances:

```
using System;

public class Panda
{
  public string Name;            // Instance field
  public static int Population;   // Static field

  public Panda (string n)      // Constructor
  {
    Name = n;                   // Assign instance field
    Population = Population+1; // Increment static field
  }
}
```

The following code creates two instances of the Panda, prints their names and then the total population:

```
Panda p1 = new Panda ("Pan Dee");
Panda p2 = new Panda ("Pan Dah");

Console.WriteLine (p1.Name);      // Pan Dee
Console.WriteLine (p2.Name);      // Pan Dah

Console.WriteLine (Panda.Population);    // 2
```

The public keyword

The public keyword exposes members to other classes. In this example, if the Name field in Panda was not public, the Test class could not access it. Marking a member public is how a type communicates: "Here is what I want other types to see—everything else is my own private implementation details." In object-oriented terms, we say that the public members *encapsulate* the private members of the class.

Conversions

C# can convert between instances of compatible types, through *implicit* and *explicit* conversions. A conversion always creates a new value from an existing one. Conversions can be either implicit or explicit; implicit conversions happen automatically, and explicit conversions require a *cast*. In the following example, we implicitly cast an int to a long type (which has twice the capacity of an int) and *explicitly* cast an int to a short type (which has half the capacity of an int):

```
int x = 123456;    // int is a 32-bit integer
long y = x;        // Implicit conversion to 64-bit int
short z = (short)x; // Explicit conversion to 16-bit int
```

Implicit conversions are allowed when:

- The compiler can guarantee they will always succeed, *and* no information is lost in conversion.

Conversely, *explicit* conversions are required when:

- The compiler cannot guarantee they will always succeed, *or* information may be lost during conversion.

False— see float to integral

Most conversions are built into the language, such as the previously shown numeric conversions. Occasionally, it is useful to write *custom conversions* (see the upcoming "Operator Overloading" section).

Value Types Versus Reference Types

All C# types fall into the following categories:

- Value types
- Reference types
- Pointer types

Value types comprise most built-in types (specifically, all numeric types, the char type, and the bool type) as well as custom struct and enum types.

Reference types comprise all class, array, delegate, and interface types.

The fundamental difference between value types and reference types is how they are handled in memory. Pointer types fall outside mainstream C# usage (see the upcoming "Unsafe Code and Pointers" section).

Value types

The content of a *value type* variable or constant is simply a value. For example, the content of the built-in value type int is 32 bits of data.

You can define a custom value type with the struct keyword as follows (see Figure 1).

```
public struct Point { public int X, Y; }
```

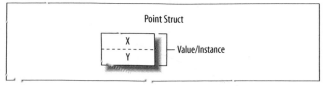

Figure 1. A value type instance in memory

The assignment of a value type instance always *copies* the instance. For example:

```
Point p1 = new Point();
p1.X = 7;

Point p2 = p1;                 // Assignment causes copy

Console.WriteLine (p1.X);   // 7
Console.WriteLine (p2.X);   // 7

p1.X = 9;                      // Change p1.X

Console.WriteLine (p1.X);   // 9
Console.WriteLine (p2.X);   // 7
```

Figure 2 shows that p1 and p2 have independent storage.

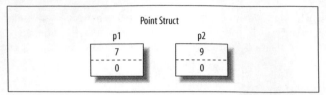

Figure 2. Assignment copies a value type instance

Reference types

A reference type is more complex than a value type, having two parts: an *object* and the *reference* to that object. The content of a reference type variable or constant is a reference to an object that contains the value. Here is the Point type from our previous example rewritten as a class, rather than a struct (see Figure 3).

```
public class Point { public int X, Y; }
```

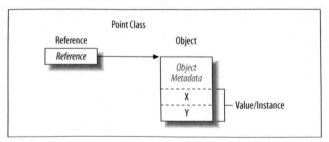

Figure 3. A reference type instance in memory

Assigning a reference type variable copies the reference, not the object instance. This allows multiple variables to refer to the same object—something not ordinarily possible with value types. If we repeat the previous example, but with Point now a class, an operation to X affects Y:

```
Point p1 = new Point( );
p1.X = 7;

Point p2 = p1;              // Copies p1 reference

Console.WriteLine (p1.X);   // 7
Console.WriteLine (p2.X);   // 7

p1.X = 9;                   // Change p1.X

Console.WriteLine (p1.X);   // 9
Console.WriteLine (p2.X);   // 9
```

Figure 4 shows that p1 and p2 are two references that point to
the same object.

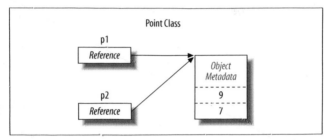

Figure 4. Assignment copies a reference

Null

A reference can be assigned the literal null, indicating that
the reference points to no object:

```
class Point {...}
...

Point p = null;
Console.WriteLine (p == null);  // True

// The following line generates a runtime
// error (a NullReferenceException is thrown):
Console.WriteLine (p.X);
```

In contrast, a value type cannot ordinarily have a null value:

```
struct Point {...}
...

Point p = null;   // Compile-time error
int x = null;     // Compile-time error
```

NOTE

C# has a construct called *nullable types* for representing value-type nulls (see the later "Nullable Types" section).

Storage overhead

Value type instances occupy precisely the sum of the memory occupied by their fields.

Reference types require separate allocations of memory for the reference and object. The object consumes as many bytes as its fields, plus additional administrative overhead (typically 12 bytes). Each reference to an object requires an extra 4 or 8 bytes, depending on whether the .NET runtime is running on a 32- or 64-bit platform.

Predefined Type Taxonomy

The following are the predefined types in C#:

Value types
  - Numeric types
    — Signed integer (sbyte, short, int, long)
    — Unsigned integer (byte, ushort, uint, ulong)
    — Real number (float, double, decimal)
  - Logical (bool)
  - Character (char)

Reference types
  - String (string)
  - Object (object)

Predefined types in C# alias Framework types in the System namespace. There is only a syntactic difference between these two statements:

```
int i = 5;
System.Int32 i = 5;
```

The predefined value types are also known as *primitive types*. Primitive types are so called because they are the atoms, or smallest possible building blocks of data, in a language, and most have a direct representation in machine code.

Numeric Types

C# has the following predefined numeric types.

C# type	System type	Suffix	Size	Range
Integral —signed				
sbyte	SByte		8 bits	-2^7 to 2^7-1
short	Int16		16 bits	-2^{15} to $2^{15}-1$
int	Int32		32 bits	-2^{31} to $2^{31}-1$
long	Int64	L	64 bits	-2^{63} to $2^{63}-1$
Integral—unsigned				
byte	Byte		8 bits	0 to 2^8-1
ushort	UInt16		16 bits	0 to $2^{16}-1$
uint	UInt32	U	32 bits	0 to $2^{32}-1$
ulong	UInt64	UL	64 bits	0 to $2^{64}-1$
Real				
float	Single	F	32 bits	$\pm(\sim 10^{-45}$ to $10^{38})$
double	Double	D	64 bits	$\pm(\sim 10^{-324}$ to $10^{308})$
decimal	Decimal	M	128 bits	$\pm(\sim 10^{-28}$ to $10^{28})$

Of the *integral* types, int and long are first-class citizens and C# and the runtime favor both. The other integral types are typically used for interoperability or when space efficiency is paramount.

Of the *real* number types, float and double are called *floating-point types* [*] and are typically used for scientific calculations. The decimal type is typically used for financial calculations, where base-10-accurate arithmetic and high precision are required.

Numeric Literals

Integral literals can use decimal or hexadecimal notation; hexadecimal is denoted with the 0x prefix. For example:

```
int x = 127;
long y = 0x7F;
```

Real literals can use decimal and/or exponential notation. For example:

```
double d = 1.5;
double million = 1E06;
```

Numeric literal type inference

By default, the compiler *infers* a numeric literal to be either double or an integral type:

- If the literal contains a decimal point or the exponential symbol (E), it is a double.
- Otherwise, the literal's type is the first type in this list that can fit the literal's value: int, uint, ulong, and long.

For example:

```
Console.Write(        1.0.GetType());  // Double (double)
Console.Write(       1E06.GetType());  // Double (double)
Console.Write(          1.GetType());  // Int32 (int)
Console.Write(0xF0000000.GetType());  // UInt32 (uint)
```

---

[*] Technically, decimal is a floating-point type too, although it's not referred to as such in the C# language specification.

Numeric suffixes

Numeric suffixes explicitly define the type of a literal (suffixes can be either lower- or uppercase):

Category	C# type	Notes	Example
F	float		float f = 1.0F;
D	double		double d = 1D;
M	decimal		decimal d = 1.0M;
U	uint or ulong	Combinable with L	uint i = 1U;
L	long or ulong	Combinable with U	ulong i = 1UL;

The suffixes U and L are rarely necessary because the uint, long, and ulong types can nearly always be either *inferred* or *implicitly converted* from int:

```
long i = 5;    // implicit lossless conversion from
               // int literal to long
```

The D suffix is technically redundant, in that all literals with a decimal point are inferred to be double. And you can always add a decimal point to a numeric literal:

```
double x = 4.0;
```

The F and M suffixes are the most useful and should always be applied when specifying float or decimal literals. Without the F suffix, the following line would not compile because 4.5 would be inferred to be of type double, which has no implicit conversion to float:

```
float f = 4.5F;
```

The same principle is true for a decimal literal:

```
decimal x = -1.23M;    // Will not compile without
                       // the M suffix.
```

The semantics of numeric conversions are described in detail in the following section.

Numeric Conversions

Integral to integral conversions

Integral conversions are *implicit* when the destination type can represent every possible value of the source type. Otherwise, an *explicit* conversion is required.

Floating-point to floating-point conversions

A float can be implicitly converted to a double, as a double can represent every possible value of a float. The reverse conversion must be explicit.

Floating-point to integral conversions

All integral types may be implicitly converted to all floating-point numbers:

```
int i = 1;
float f = i;
```

The reverse conversion must be explicit:

```
int i2 = (int)f;
```

WARNING

When you cast from a floating-point number to an integral, any fractional portion is truncated; no rounding is performed. The static class System.Convert provides methods that round while converting between various numeric types.

Implicitly converting a large integral type to a floating-point type preserves *magnitude* but may occasionally lose *precision*. This is because floating-point types always have more magnitude than integral types, but they may have less precision. Rewriting our example with a larger number demonstrates:

```
int i1 = 100000001;
float f = i1;      // Magnitude preserved, precision lost
int i2 = (int)f;   // 100000000
```

Decimal conversions

All integral types can be implicitly converted to the decimal type because a decimal can represent every possible C# integral value. All other numeric conversions to and from a decimal type must be explicit.

Arithmetic Operators

The arithmetic operators (+, -, *, /, %) are defined for all numeric types except the 8- and 16-bit integral types:

```
+    Addition
-    Subtraction
*    Multiplication
/    Division
%    Remainder after division
```

Increment and Decrement Operators

The increment and decrement operators (++, --) increment and decrement numeric types by one. The operator can either precede or follow the variable, depending on whether you want the variable to be updated *before* or *after* the expression is evaluated. For example:

```
int x = 0;
Console.WriteLine (x++);   // outputs 0; x is now 1
Console.WriteLine (++x);   // outputs 2; x is now 2
Console.WriteLine (--x);   // outputs 1; x is now 1
```

Specialized Integral Operations

Integral division

Division operations on integral types always truncate remainders. Dividing by a variable whose value is 0 generates a runtime error (a DivisionByZeroException). Dividing by the literal 0 generates a compile-time error.

Integral overflow

At runtime, arithmetic operations on integral types can overflow. By default, this happens silently—no exception is thrown. While the C# specification is agnostic as to the result of an overflow, the CLR always causes wraparound behavior. For example, decrementing the minimum possible int value results in the maximum possible int value:

```
int a = int.MinValue;
a--;
Console.WriteLine (a == int.MaxValue); // True
```

Integral arithmetic overflow check operators

The checked operator tells the runtime to generate an OverflowException rather than failing silently when an integral expression or statement exceeds the arithmetic limits of that type. The checked operator affects expressions with the ++, --, (unary) -, +, -, *, /, and explicit conversion operators between integral types.

checked can be used around either an expression or a statement block. For example:

```
int a = 1000000, b = 1000000;

int c = checked (a*b);     // Checks just the expression

checked                    // Checks all expressions
{                          // in statement block
   c = a * b;
   ...
}
```

You can make arithmetic overflow checking the default for all expressions in a program by compiling with the /checked+ command-line switch (in Visual Studio, go to Advanced Build Settings). If you then need to disable overflow checking just for specific expressions or statements, you can do so with the unchecked operator.

Overflow checking for constant expressions

Regardless of the /checked compiler switch, expressions evaluated at compile time are always overflow-checked—unless you apply the unchecked operator:

```
int x = int.MaxValue + 1;            // Compile-time error
int y = unchecked (int.MaxValue + 1);     // No errors
```

Bitwise operators

C# supports these standard C-style bitwise operations.

Operator	Meaning	Sample expression	Result
~	Complement	~0xfU	0xfffffff0U
&	And	0xf0 & 0x33	0x30
|	Or	0xf0 | 0x33	0xf3
^	Exclusive Or	0xff00 ^ 0x0ff0	0xf0f0
<<	Shift left	0x20 << 2	0x80
>>	Shift right	0x20 >> 1	0x10

8- and 16-Bit Integrals

The 8- and 16-bit integral types are byte, sbyte, short, and ushort. These types lack their own arithmetic operators, so C# implicitly converts them to larger types as required. This can cause a compile-time error when trying to assign the result back to a small integral type:

```
short x = 1, y = 1;
short z = x + y;            // Compile-time error
```

In this case, x and y are implicitly converted to int so that the addition can be performed. This means the result is also an int, which cannot be implicitly cast back to a short (because it could cause loss of data). To make this compile, we must add an explicit cast:

```
short z = (short) (x + y);    // OK
```

Special Float and Double Values

Unlike integral types, floating-point types have values that certain operations treat specially. These special values are NaN (Not a Number), +∞, −∞, and −0. The float and double classes have constants for NaN, +∞, and −∞, as well as other values (MaxValue, MinValue, and Epsilon). For example:

```
Console.Write (double.NegativeInfinity);  // -Infinity
```

The constants that represent special values for double and float are as follows.

Special value	Double constant	Float constant
NaN	double.NaN	float.NaN
+∞	double.PositiveInfinity	float.PositiveInfinity
−∞	double.NegativeInfinity	float.NegativeInfinity
−0	-0.0	-0.0f

Dividing a nonzero number by zero results in an infinite value. For example:

```
Console.WriteLine ( 1.0 /  0.0);       //  Infinity
Console.WriteLine (-1.0 /  0.0);       // -Infinity
Console.WriteLine ( 1.0 / -0.0);       // -Infinity
Console.WriteLine (-1.0 / -0.0);       //  Infinity
```

Dividing zero by zero, or subtracting infinity from infinity, results in a NaN. For example:

```
Console.WriteLine ( 0.0 /  0.0);              //  NaN
Console.WriteLine ((1.0 /  0.0) - (1.0 / 0.0)); //  NaN
```

When using ==, a NaN value is never equal to another value, even another NaN value:

```
Console.WriteLine (0.0 / 0.0 == double.NaN);  // False
```

To test whether a value is NaN, you must use the float. IsNaN or double.IsNaN method, as follows:

```
Console.WriteLine (double.IsNaN (0.0 / 0.0)); // True
```

When using object.Equals, however, two NaN values are equal:

```
Console.WriteLine
  (object.Equals (0.0 / 0.0, double.NaN));     // True
```

double Versus decimal

double is useful for scientific computations (such as computing spatial coordinates); decimal is useful for financial computations.

Category	double	decimal
Internal representation	Base 2	Base 10
Precision	15-16 significant figures	28-29 significant figures
Range	$\pm(\sim10^{-324}$ to $\sim10^{308})$	$\pm(\sim10^{-28}$ to $\sim10^{28})$
Special values	+0, −0, +∞, −∞, and NaN	None
Speed	Native to processor	Nonnative to processor (about 10 times slower than double)

Real Number Rounding Errors

float and double internally represent numbers in base 2. For this reason, only numbers expressible in base 2 are represented precisely. Practically, this means most literals with a fractional component (which are in base 10) will not be represented precisely. For example:

```
float tenth = 0.1f;                  // Not quite 0.1
float one   = 1f;
Console.WriteLine (one - tenth * 10f); // -1.490116E-08
```

This is why float and double are bad for financial calculations. In contrast, decimal works in base 10 and so can precisely represent numbers expressible in base 10 (as well as its factors, base 2 and base 5). Because real literals are in base 10, decimal can precisely represent numbers such as 0.1. However, neither double nor decimal can precisely represent a fractional number whose base-10 representation is recurring:

```
decimal m = 1M / 6M;   // 0.1666666666666666666666666667M
double  d = 1.0 / 6.0;      // 0.16666666666666666
```

This leads to accumulated rounding errors:

```
decimal notQuiteWholeM =
    m+m+m+m+m+m;        // 1.0000000000000000000000000002M
double notQuiteWholeD =
    d+d+d+d+d+d;        // 0.99999999999999989
```

which breaks equality and comparison operations:

```
Console.WriteLine (notQuiteWholeM == 1M);   // False
Console.WriteLine (notQuiteWholeD < 1.0);   // True
```

Boolean Type and Operators

C#'s bool type (aliasing the System.Boolean type) is a logical value that can be assigned the literal true or false.

Although a Boolean value requires only one bit (zero or one) of storage, the runtime will use one or two bytes of memory, as this is the minimum chunk that the runtime and processor can efficiently work with. To avoid space-inefficiency in the case of arrays, the Framework provides a BitArray class in the System.Collections namespace, which is designed to use just one bit per Boolean value.

Equality and Comparison Operators

== and != test for equality and inequality of any type, but always return a bool value. Value types typically have a very simple notion of equality:

```
int x = 1, y = 2, z = 1;
Console.WriteLine (x == y);      // False
Console.WriteLine (x == z);      // True
```

For reference types, equality, by default, is based on *reference*, as opposed to the actual *value* of the underlying object:

```
public class Dude
{
  public string Name;
  public Dude (string n) { Name = n; }
}

Dude d1 = new Dude ("John");
Dude d2 = new Dude ("John");
Console.WriteLine (d1 == d2);      // False
Dude d3 = d1;
Console.WriteLine (d1 == d3);      // True
```

The comparison operators, <, >, <=, and >=, work for all numeric types, but should be used with caution with real numbers (see the previous section "Real Number Rounding Errors"). The comparison operators also work on enum type members, by comparing their underlying integral values.

We'll explain the equality and comparison operators in greater detail, later, in the "The object Type" and "Operator Overloading" sections.

Conditional Operators

The && and || operators test for *and* and *or* conditions. They are frequently used in conjunction with the ! operator, which expresses *not*. In this example, the UseUmbrella method returns true if it's rainy or sunny (to protect us from the rain or the sun), as long as it's not also windy (as umbrellas are useless in the wind):

```
static bool UseUmbrella (bool rainy, bool sunny,
                         bool windy)
{
  return ! windy && (rainy || sunny);
}
```

Conditional operators *short-circuit* evaluation when possible. In the preceding example, if it is windy, the expression (rainy || sunny) is not even evaluated.

WARNING

The & and | operators can be used in a similar manner:

```
return ! windy & (rainy | sunny);
```

The difference is that they *do not short-circuit*. For this reason, they are rarely used in place of conditional operators.

The ternary conditional operator has the form q ? a : b, where if condition q is true, a is evaluated, else b is evaluated. For example:

```
static int Max (int a, int b)
{
  return (a > b) ? a : b;
}
```

Strings and Characters

C#'s char type (aliasing the System.Char type) represents a Unicode character, and it occupies two bytes. A char literal is specified inside single quotes:

```
char c = 'A';        // simple character
```

Escape sequences express characters that cannot be expressed or interpreted literally. An escape sequence is a backslash followed by a character with a special meaning. For example:

```
char newLine = '\n';
char backSlash = '\\';
```

The escape sequence characters are outlined below.

Char	Meaning	Value
\'	Single quote	0x0027
\"	Double quote	0x0022

Char	Meaning	Value
\\	Backslash	0x005C
\0	Null	0x0000
\a	Alert	0x0007
\b	Backspace	0x0008
\f	Form feed	0x000C
\n	New line	0x000A
\r	Carriage return	0x000D
\t	Horizontal tab	0x0009
\v	Vertical tab	0x000B

The \u (or \x) escape sequence lets you specify any Unicode character via its four-digit hexadecimal code:

```
char copyrightSymbol = '\u00A9';
char omegaSymbol     = '\u03A9';
char newLine         = '\u000A';
```

Char Conversions

An implicit conversion from a char to a numeric type works for the numeric types that can accommodate an unsigned short. For other numeric types, an explicit conversion is required.

String Type

C#'s string type (aliasing the System.String type) represents an immutable sequence of Unicode characters. A string literal is specified inside double quotes:

```
string a = "Heat";
```

NOTE

string is a reference type, not a value type. Its equality operators, however, implement value-type semantics.

The escape sequences that are valid for char literals also work inside strings:

```
string a = "Here's a tab:\t";
```

The cost being that whenever you need a literal backslash, you must write it twice:

```
string a1 = "\\\\server\\fileshare\\helloworld.cs";
```

To avoid this problem, C# allows *verbatim* string literals. A verbatim string literal is prefixed with @ and does not support escape sequences. The following verbatim string is identical to the preceding one:

```
string a2 = @"\\server\fileshare\helloworld.cs";
```

A verbatim string literal can also span multiple lines:

```
string escaped  = "First Line\r\nSecond Line";
string verbatim = @"First Line
Second Line";

Console.WriteLine (escaped == verbatim);  // True
```

You can include the double-quote character in a verbatim literal by writing it twice:

```
string xml = @"<customer id=""123""></customer>";
```

String concatenation

The + operator concatenates two strings:

```
string s = "a" + "b";
```

The righthand operand may be a non-string value, in which case ToString is called on that value. For example:

```
string s = "a" + 5;  // a5
```

Because string is immutable, using the + operator repeatedly to build up a string can be inefficient. The solution is to instead use the System.Text.StringBuilder type—this represents a mutable (editable) string, and it has methods to efficiently Append, Insert, Remove, and Replace substrings.

String comparisons

string does not support < and > operators for comparisons. You must instead use string's CompareTo method, which returns a positive number, a negative number, or zero, depending on whether the first value comes after, before, or alongside the second value:

```
Console.Write ("Boston".CompareTo ("Austin"));   // 1
Console.Write ("Boston".CompareTo ("Boston"));   // 0
Console.Write ("Boston".CompareTo ("Chicago"));  // -1
```

Searching within strings

String's indexer returns a character at a specified position:

```
Console.Write ("word"[2]);   // r
```

The IndexOf/LastIndexOf methods search for a character within the string; the Contains, StartsWith, and EndWith methods search for a substring within the string.

Manipulating strings

Because String is immutable, all the methods that "manipulate" a string return a new one, leaving the original untouched:

- Substring extracts a portion of a string.
- Insert and Remove insert and remove characters at a specified position.
- PadLeft and PadRight add whitespace.
- TrimStart, TrimEnd, and Trim remove whitespace.

The string class also defines ToUpper and ToLower methods for changing case, a Split method to split a string into substrings (based on supplied delimiters), and a static Join method to join substrings back into a string.

Arrays

An array represents a fixed number of elements of a particular type. The elements in an array are always stored in a contiguous block of memory, providing highly efficient access.

An array is denoted with square brackets after the element type. For example:

```
char[] vowels = new char[5];   // Declare an array of 5
characters
```

Square brackets also *index* the array, accessing a particular element by position:

```
vowels [0] = 'a';
vowels [1] = 'e';
vowels [2] = 'i';
vowels [3] = 'o';
vowels [4] = 'u';
Console.WriteLine (vowels [1]);      // e
```

This prints "e" because array indexes start at zero. We can use a for loop statement to iterate through each element in the array. The for loop in this example cycles the integer i from 0 to 4:

```
for (int i = 0; i < vowels.Length; i++)
  Console.Write (vowels [i]);          // aeiou
```

Arrays also implement IEnumerable<T>, so you can enumerate members with the foreach statement:

```
foreach (char c in vowels) Console.Write (c);  // aeiou
```

The Length property of an array returns the number of elements in the array. Once an array has been created, its length cannot be changed. The System.Collection namespace and subnamespaces provide higher-level data structures, such as dynamically sized arrays and dictionaries.

An *array initialization expression* specifies each element of an array. For example:

```
char[] vowels = new char[] {'a','e','i','o','u'};
```

All arrays inherit from the System.Array class, which defines common methods and properties for all arrays. This includes instance properties such as Length and Rank, and static methods to:

- Dynamically create an array (CreateInstance)
- Get and set elements regardless of the array type (GetValue/SetValue)
- Search a sorted array (BinarySearch) or an unsorted array (IndexOf, LastIndexOf, Find, FindIndex, FindLastIndex)
- Sort an array (Sort)
- Copy an array (Copy)

Default Element Initialization

Creating an array always preinitializes the elements with default values. The default value for a type is the result of a bitwise-zeroing of memory. For example, consider creating an array of integers. Because int is a value type, it allocates 1,000 integers in one contiguous block of memory. The default value for each element will be 0:

```
int[] a = new int[1000];
Console.Write (a[123]);          // 0
```

Value types versus reference types

Whether an array element type is a value type or a reference type has important performance implications. When the element type is a value type, each element value is allocated as part of the array. For example:

```
public struct Point { public int X, Y; }
...

Point[] a = new Point[1000];
int x = a[500].X;                // 0
```

Had Point been a class, creating the array would have merely allocated 1,000 null references:

```
public class Point { public int X, Y; }

...
Point[] a = new Point[1000];
int x = a[500].X;           // Runtime error
                            // (NullReferenceException)
```

To avoid this error, we must manually instantiate 1,000 Point objects after instantiating the array:

```
Point[] a = new Point[1000];
for (int i = 0; i < a.Length; i++) // Iterate i from
                                   // 0 to 999
  a[i] = new Point();              // Set array element
                                   // i with new point
```

An array *itself* is always a reference type object, regardless of element type:

```
int[] a = null;    // Legal - int[] is reference type
```

Multidimensional Arrays

Multidimensional arrays come in two varieties: rectangular and jagged. Rectangular arrays represent an *n*-dimensional block of memory, and jagged arrays are arrays of arrays.

Rectangular arrays

Rectangular arrays are declared using commas to separate each dimension. The following declares a rectangular two-dimensional array, where the dimensions are 3 by 3:

```
int[,] matrix = new int [3, 3];
```

The GetLength method of an array returns the length for a given dimension (starting at 0):

```
for (int i = 0; i < matrix.GetLength (0); i++)
  for (int j = 0; j < matrix.GetLength (1); j++)
    matrix [i, j] = i * 3 + j;
```

A rectangular array can be initialized as follows (each element in this example is initialized to be identical to the previous example):

```
int[,] matrix = new int[,]
{
  {0,1,2},
  {3,4,5},
  {6,7,8}
};
```

Jagged arrays

Jagged arrays are declared using successive square brackets to represent each dimension. Here is an example of declaring a jagged two-dimensional array, where the outermost dimension is 3:

```
int [][] matrix = new int [3][];
```

The inner dimensions aren't specified in the declaration. Unlike a rectangular array, each inner array can be an arbitrary length. Each inner array is implicitly initialized to null rather than an empty array. Each inner array must be created manually:

```
for (int i = 0; i < matrix.Length; i++)
{
  matrix[i] = new int [3];          // create inner array
  for (int j = 0; j < matrix[i].Length; j++)
    matrix[i][j] = i * 3 + j;
}
```

A jagged array can be initialized as follows (each element in this example is initialized to be identical to the previous example):

```
int[][] matrix = new int[][]
{
  new int[] {0,1,2},
  new int[] {3,4,5},
  new int[] {6,7,8}
};
```

Simplified Array Initialization Expressions

There are two ways to shorten array initialization expressions; the first is to omit the new operator and type qualifications:

```
char[] vowels = {'a','e','i','o','u'};

int[,]rectangularMatrix =
{
  {0,1,2},
  {3,4,5},
  {6,7,8}
};

int[][]jaggedMatrix =
{
  new int[] {0,1,2},
  new int[] {3,4,5},
  new int[] {6,7,8}
};
```

In C# 3.0, the second approach is to use the var keyword, which tells the compiler to implicitly type a local variable:

```
var i = 3;          // i is implicitly of type int
var s = "sausage";  // s is implicitly of type string

// Therefore:

var rectMatrix = new int[,] // rectMatrix is implicitly
{                           // of type int[,]
  {0,1,2},
  {3,4,5},
  {6,7,8}
};

var jaggedMat = new int[][] // jaggedMat is implicitly
{                           // of type int[][]
  new int[] {0,1,2},
  new int[] {3,4,5},
  new int[] {6,7,8}
};
```

Implicit typing can be taken one stage further with single-dimensional arrays. You can omit the type qualifier after the new keyword, and have the compiler *infer* the array type:

```
// Compiler infers char[]

var vowels = new[] {'a','e','i','o','u'};
```

The elements must have identical types for implicit array typing to work. For example:

```
var x = new[] {1, "a"};    // Error, elements are of
                           // multiple types
```

Bounds Checking

All array indexing is bounds-checked by the runtime. An IndexOutOfRangeException is thrown if you use an invalid index:

```
int[] arr = new int[3];
arr[3] = 1;                // IndexOutOfRangeException thrown
```

Like with Java, array bounds checking is necessary for type safety, and it simplifies debugging.

NOTE

Generally, the performance hit from bounds checking is minor, and the JIT (Just-in-Time compiler) can perform optimizations, such as determining in advance whether all indices will be safe before entering a loop, thus avoiding a check on each iteration. In addition, C# provides "unsafe" code that can explicitly bypass bounds checking (see the upcoming "Unsafe Code and Pointers" section).

Variables and Parameters

A variable represents a storage location that has a modifiable value. A variable can be a *local variable*, *parameter* (*value*, *ref*, or *out*), *field* (*instance* or *static*), or *array element*.

The Stack and the Heap

The stack and the heap are the places where variables and constants reside. Each has very different lifetime semantics.

Stack

The stack is a block of memory for storing local variables and parameters. The stack automatically grows and shrinks as a function is entered and exited. Consider the following method (to avoid distraction, input argument checking is ignored):

```
static int Factorial (int x)
{
  if (x == 0) return 1;
  return x * Factorial (x-1);
}
```

This method is recursive, meaning that it calls itself. Each time the method is entered, a new `int` is allocated on the stack, and each time the method exits, the `int` is deallocated.

Heap

The heap is a block of memory in which *objects* (i.e., reference type instances) reside. Whenever a new object is created, it is allocated on the heap, and a reference to that object is returned. During a program's execution, the heap starts filling up as new objects are created. The runtime has a garbage collector that periodically deallocates objects from the heap, so your computer does not run out of memory. An object is eligible for deallocation as soon as nothing references it. In the following example, the `StringBuilder` object is created on the heap, while the `sb` *reference* is created on the stack:

```
static void Test( )
{
  StringBuilder sb = new StringBuilder( );
  Console.WriteLine (sb.Length);
}
```

After the Test method finishes, sb pops off the stack, and the StringBuilder object is no longer referenced, so it becomes eligible for garbage collection.

Value type instances (and object references) live wherever the variable was declared. If the instance was declared as a field within an object, or as an array element, that instance lives on the heap.

NOTE

You can't explicitly delete objects in C#, as you can in C++. An unreferenced object is eventually collected by the garbage collector.

You can't explicitly delete objects in C#, as you can in C++. An unreferenced object is eventually collected by the garbage collector. The heap is also used to store static fields and constants. Unlike objects allocated on the heap (which can get garbage collected), these will live until the application domain is torn down.

Definite Assignment

C# enforces a definite assignment policy. In practice, this means that outside of an unsafe context, it's impossible to access uninitialized memory. Definite assignment has three implications:

- Local variables must be assigned a value before they can be read.
- Function arguments must be supplied when a method is called.
- All other variables (such as fields and array elements) are automatically initialized by the runtime.

For example, the following code results in a compile-time error:

```
static void Main()
{
  int x;
  Console.WriteLine (x);        // compile-time error
}
```

Fields and array elements are automatically initialized with the default values for their type. The following code outputs 0 because array elements are implicitly assigned to their default values:

```
static void Main()
{
  int[] ints = new int[2];
  Console.WriteLine (ints[0]);              // 0
}
```

The following code outputs 0 because fields are implicitly assigned to a default value:

```
class Test
{
  static int x;
  static void Main() { Console.WriteLine (x); }  // 0
}
```

Default Values

All type instances have a default value. The default value for the primitives is the result of a bitwise-zeroing of memory.

Type	Default value
Reference	null
Numeric type or enum type	0
char type	'\0'
bool type	false

The default value in a custom value type (i.e., struct) is the same as the default value for each field defined by the custom type.

Parameters

A method has a sequence of parameters. Parameters define the set of arguments that must be provided for that method. In this example, the method Foo has a single parameter named p, of type int:

```
static void Foo (int p)
{
  p = p + 1;                 // increment p by 1
  Console.WriteLine(p);      // write p to screen
}
static void Main() { Foo(8); }
```

You can control how parameters are passed with the ref and out modifiers.

Parameter modifier	Passed by	Variable must be definitely assigned
None	Value	Going *in*
ref	Reference	Going *in*
out	Reference	Going *out*

Passing arguments by value

By default, arguments in C# are *passed by value*, which is by far the most common case. This means a copy of the value is created when passed to the method:

```
class Test
{
  static void Foo (int p)
  {
    p = p + 1;                 // Increment p by 1
    Console.WriteLine (p);     // Write p to screen
  }

  static void Main()
  {
    int x = 8;
    Foo (x);                   // Make a copy of x
    Console.WriteLine (x);     // x will still be 8
  }
}
```

Assigning p a new value does not change the contents of x because p and x reside in different memory locations.

Passing a reference type object by value copies the *reference*, but not the object. In the following example, Foo sees the same StringBuilder object that Main instantiated, but has an independent reference to it. In other words, sb and fooSB are separate variables that reference the same StringBuilder object:

```
class Test
{
  static void Foo (StringBuilder fooSB)
  {
    fooSB.Append ("test");
    fooSB = null;
  }

  static void Main()
  {
    StringBuilder sb = new StringBuilder();
    Foo (sb);
    Console.WriteLine (sb.ToString());    // test
  }
}
```

Because fooSB is a *copy* of a reference, setting it to null doesn't make sb null. (If, however, fooSB was declared and called with the ref modifier, sb *would* become null.)

The ref modifier

To *pass by reference*, C# provides the ref parameter modifier. In the following example, p and x refer to the same memory locations:

```
class Test
{
  static void Foo (ref int p)
  {
    p = p + 1;                 // increment p by 1
    Console.WriteLine(p);      // write p to screen
  }
```

```
static void Main()
{
  int x = 8;
  Foo (ref x);            // Ask Foo to deal directly
                          // with x
  Console.WriteLine(x);   // x is now 9
}
}
```

Now assigning p a new value changes the contents of x. Notice how the ref modifier is required both when writing and when calling the method. This makes it very clear what's going on.

NOTE

A parameter can be passed by reference or by value, regardless of whether the parameter type is a reference type or a value type.

The out modifier

An out argument is like a ref argument, except it:

- Need not be assigned before it goes into the function
- Must be assigned before it comes *out* of the function

The out modifier is most commonly used to get multiple return values back from a method. Like a ref parameter, an out parameter is passed by reference.

Implications of passing by reference

When you pass an argument by reference, you alias the storage location of an existing variable, rather than creating a new storage location. In the following example, the variables x and y represent the same instance:

```
class Test
{
  static int x;

  static void Main() { Foo (out x); }
```

```
  static void Foo (out int y)
  {
    Console.WriteLine (x);        // x is 0
    y = 1;                        // Mutate y
    Console.WriteLine (x);        // x is 1
  }
}
```

The params modifier

The params modifier may be specified on the last parameter of a method so that the method accepts any number of parameters of a particular type. The parameter type must be declared as an array. For example:

```
static int Sum (params int[] ints)
{
  int sum = 0;
  for (int i = 0; i < ints.Length; i++)
    sum += ints[i];        // increase sum by ints[i]
  return sum;
}

static void Main()
{
  int total = Sum (1, 2, 3, 4);
  Console.WriteLine (total);        // 10
}
```

You can also supply a params argument as an ordinary array. The first line in Main is semantically equivalent to this:

```
int total = Sum (new int[] { 1, 2, 3, 4 } );
```

var: Implicitly Typed Local Variables (C# 3.0)

It is often the case that you declare and initialize a variable in one step. If the compiler is able to infer the type from the initialization expression, you can use the word var in place of the type declaration. For example:

```
var x = 5;
var y = "hello";
var z = new System.Text.StringBuilder();
var req = (System.Net.FtpWebRequest)
          System.Net.WebRequest.Create ("...");
```

This is precisely equivalent to:

```
int    x = 5;
string y = "hello";

System.Text.StringBuilder z =
  new System.Text.StringBuilder();

System.Net.FtpWebRequest req =
  (System.Net.FtpWebRequest)
  System.Net.WebRequest.Create ("...");
```

Because of this direct equivalence, implicitly typed variables are statically typed. For example, the following generates a compile-time error:

```
var x = 5;
x = "hello";    // Compile-time error; x is of type int
```

NOTE

var can decrease code readability in the case *you can't deduce the type purely from looking at the variable declaration*. For example:

```
Random r = new Random();
var x = r.Next();
```

What type is x?

In the upcoming section "Anonymous Types (C# 3.0)," we describe a scenario in which the use of var is mandatory.

Expressions and Operators

An *expression* essentially denotes a value. The simplest kinds of expressions are constants and variables. Expressions can be transformed and combined using operators. An *operator* takes one or more input *operands* to output a new expression.

Here is an example of a *constant expression*:

```
12
```

We can use the * operator to combine two operands (the literal expressions 12 and 30), as follows:

```
12 * 30
```

Complex expressions can be built because an operand may itself be an expression, such as the operand (12 * 30) in the following example:

```
1 + (12 * 30)
```

Operators in C# are classed as *unary*, *binary*, or *ternary*—depending on the number of operands they work on (one, two, or three). The binary operators always use *infix* notation, where the operator is placed *between* the two operands.

Primary Expressions

Primary expressions include expressions composed of operators that are intrinsic to the basic plumbing of the language. Here is an example:

```
Math.Log (1)
```

This expression is composed of two primary expressions. The first expression performs a member-lookup (with the . operator), and the second expression performs a method call (with the ( ) operator).

Void Expressions

A *void expression* is an expression that has no value. For example:

```
Console.WriteLine (1)
```

A void expression—because it has no value—cannot be used as an operand to build more complex expressions:

```
1 + Console.WriteLine(1)      // Compile-time error
```

Assignment Expressions

An assignment expression uses the = operator to assign a variable the result of another expression. For example:

```
x = x * 5
```

An assignment expression is not a void expression. It actually carries the assignment value and thus can be incorporated into another expression. In the following example, the expression assigns 2 to x and 10 to y:

```
y = 5 * (x = 2)
```

This style of expression can be used to initialize multiple values:

```
a = b = c = d = 0
```

The *compound assignment operators* are syntactic shortcuts that combine assignment with another operator. For example:

```
x *= 2    // equivalent to x = x * 2
x <<= 1   // equivalent to x = x << 1
```

Operator Precedence and Associativity

When an expression contains multiple operators, *precedence* and *associativity* determine the order of evaluation. Operators with higher precedence execute before operators of lower precedence. If the operators have the same precedence, the operator's associativity determines the order of evaluation.

Precedence

The following expression:

```
1 + 2 * 3
```

is evaluated as follows, as * has a higher precedence than +:

```
1 + (2 * 3)
```

Left-associative operators

Binary operators (except for assignment operators) are *left-associative*; in other words, they are evaluated from left to right. For example, the following expression:

```
8 / 4 / 2
```

is evaluated as follows due to left associativity:

```
( 8 / 4 ) / 2    // 1
```

You can insert parentheses to change the default order of evaluation:

```
8 / ( 4 / 2 )    // 4
```

Right-associative operators

The *assignment operators*, the unary operators, and the conditional operator are *right-associative*; in other words, they are evaluated from right to left. For example:

```
int x = 0;
int y = -~x;    // 1  (Complements first, then negates)
int z = ~-x;    // -1 (Negates first, then complements)
```

Operator Table

Table 1 lists C#'s operators in order of precedence. Operators in the same category have the same precedence. See the upcoming "Operator Overloading" section for information on how to overload operators.

Table 1. C# operators (categories in order of precedence)

Operator symbol	Operator name	Example	User-overloadable
Primary (highest precedence)			
( )	Grouping	while(x)	No
.	Member access	x.y	No
->	Pointer to struct (unsafe)	x->y	No
( )	Function call	x( )	No
[ ]	Array/index	a[x]	Via indexer
++	Post-increment	x++	Yes
--	Post-decrement	x--	Yes
new	Create instance	new Foo( )	No

Table 1. C# operators (categories in order of precedence) (continued)

Operator symbol	Operator name	Example	User-overloadable
stackalloc	Unsafe stack allocation	stackalloc (10)	No
typeof	Get type from identifier	typeof (int)	No
checked	Integral overflow check on	checked (x)	No
unchecked	Integral overflow check off	unchecked (x)	No
Unary			
sizeof	Get size of struct	sizeof (int)	No
+	Positive value of	+x	Yes
-	Negative value of	-x	Yes
!	Not	!x	Yes
~	Bitwise complement	~x	Yes
++	Pre-increment	++x	Yes
--	Pre-decrement	--x	Yes
( )	Cast	(int)x	No
*	Value at address (unsafe)	*x	No
&	Address of value (unsafe)	&x	No
Multiplicative			
*	Multiply	x * y	Yes
/	Divide	x / y	Yes
%	Remainder	x % y	Yes
Additive			
+	Add	x + y	Yes
-	Subtract	x - y	Yes

Table 1. C# operators (categories in order of precedence) (continued)

Operator symbol	Operator name	Example	User-overloadable
Shift			
<<	Shift left	x >> 1	Yes
>>	Shift right	x << 1	Yes
Relational			
<	Less than	x < y	Yes
>	Greater than	x > y	Yes
<=	Less than or equal to	x <= y	Yes
>=	Greater than or equal to	x >= y	Yes
is	Type is or is subclass of	x is y	No
as	Type conversion	x as y	No
Equality			
==	Equals	x == y	Yes
!=	Not equals	x != y	Yes
Logical And			
&	And	x & y	Yes
Logical Xor			
^	Exclusive Or	x ^ y	Yes
Logical Or			
		Or	x	y	Yes
Conditional And			
&&	Conditional And	x && y	Via &
Conditional Or			
||	Conditional Or	x || y	Via	
Conditional			
?:	Conditional	isTrue ? thenThis : elseThis	No

Table 1. C# operators (categories in order of precedence) (continued)

Operator symbol	Operator name	Example	User-overloadable
Assignment			
=	Assign	x = y	No
*=	Multiply self by	x *= 2	Via *
/=	Divide self by	x /= 2	Via /
+=	Add to self	x += 2	Via +
-=	Subtract from self	x -= 2	Via -
<<=	Shift self left by	x <<= 2	Via <<
>>=	Shift self right by	x >>= 2	Via >>
&=	And self by	x &= 2	Via &
^=	Exclusive-Or self by	x ^= 2	Via ^
|=	Or self by	x |= 2	Via |
Lambda (lowest precedence)			
=>	Lambda	x => x + 1	No

Statements

Functions comprise *statements* that execute sequentially in the textual order in which they appear. A *statement block* is a series of statements appearing between braces (the {} tokens).

Declaration Statements

A declaration statement declares a new variable, optionally initializing the variable with an expression. A declaration statement ends in a semicolon. You may declare multiple variables of the same type in a comma-separated list. For example:

```
string someWord = "rosebud";
int someNumber = 42;
bool rich = true, famous = false;
```

A constant declaration is like a variable declaration, except that the variable cannot be changed after it has been declared, and the initialization must occur with the declaration:

```
const double c = 2.99792458E08;
c+=10; // error
```

Local variables

The scope of a local or constant variable extends to the end of the current block. You cannot declare another local variable with the same name in the current block or in any nested blocks. For example:

```
static void Main()
{
  int x;
  {
    int y;
    int x;                  // Error, x already defined
  }
  {
    int y;                  // OK, y not in scope
  }
  Console.WriteLine(y); // Error, y is out of scope
}
```

Expression Statements

Expression statements are expressions that are also valid statements. An expression statement must either change state or call something that might change state. Changing state essentially means changing a variable. The possible expression statements are:

- Assignment expressions (including increment and decrement expressions)
- Method call expressions (both void and nonvoid)
- Object instantiation expressions

Here are some examples:

```
// Declare variables with declaration statements:
string s;
int x, y;
System.Text.StringBuilder sb;

// Expression statements
x = 1 + 2;                      // Assignment expression
x++;                            // Increment expression
y = Math.Max (x, 5);            // Assignment expression
Console.WriteLine (y);          // Method call expression
sb = new StringBuilder();       // Assignment expression
new StringBuilder();            // Object instantiation
                                // expression
```

When you call a constructor or a method that returns a
value, you're not obliged to use the result. However, unless
the constructor or method changes state the statement is
completely useless:

```
new StringBuilder();            // Legal, but does nothing
new string ('c', 3);            // Legal, but does nothing
x.Equals (y);                   // Legal, but does nothing
```

Selection Statements

C# has the following mechanisms to conditionally control
the flow of program execution:

- Selection statements (if, switch)
- Conditional operator (? :)
- Loop statements (while, do..while, for, foreach)

This section covers the simplest two constructs: the if-else
statement and the switch statement.

The if statement

An if statement executes a body of code depending on
whether a bool expression is true. For example:

```
if (5 < 2 * 3)
{
  Console.WriteLine ("true");     // true
}
```

If the body of code is a single statement, you can optionally omit the braces:

```
if (5 < 2 * 3)
  Console.WriteLine ("true");        // true
```

The else clause

An if statement is optionally followed by an else clause:

```
if (2 + 2 == 5)
  Console.WriteLine ("Does not compute");
else
  Console.WriteLine ("false");       // false
```

Within an else clause, you can nest another if statement:

```
if (2 + 2 == 5)
  Console.WriteLine ("Does not compute");
else
  if (2 + 2 == 4)
    Console.WriteLine ("Computes");   // Computes
```

Changing the flow of execution with braces

An else clause always applies to the immediately preceding if statement in the statement block. For example:

```
if (true)
  if (false)
    Console.WriteLine( );
  else
    Console.WriteLine("executes");
```

This is semantically identical to:

```
if (true)
{
  if (false)
    Console.WriteLine( );
  else
    Console.WriteLine("executes");
}
```

We can change the execution flow by moving the braces:

```
if (true)
{
  if (false)
    Console.WriteLine();
}
else
  Console.WriteLine("does not execute");
```

With braces, you explicitly state your intention. This can improve the readability of nested if statements—even when not required by the compiler. A notable exception is with the following pattern:

```
static void TellMeWhatICanDo (int age)
{
  if (age >= 35)
    Console.WriteLine ("You can be president!");
  else if (age >= 21)
    Console.WriteLine ("You can drink!");
  else if (age >= 18)
    Console.WriteLine ("You can vote!");
  else
    Console.WriteLine ("You can wait!");
}
```

Here, we've arranged the if and else statements to mimic the "elsif" construct of other languages (and C#'s #elif pre-processor directive). Visual Studio's auto-formatting recognizes this pattern and preserves the indentation. Semantically, though, each if statement following an else statement is functionally nested within the else statement.

The switch statement

switch statements let you branch program execution based on a selection of possible values a variable may have. switch statements may result in cleaner code than multiple if statements, as switch statements require an expression to be evaluated only once. For instance:

```
static void ShowCard (int cardNumber)
{
  switch (cardNumber)
  {
    case 13:
      Console.WriteLine ("King");
      break;
    case 12:
      Console.WriteLine ("Queen");
      break;
    case 11:
      Console.WriteLine ("Jack");
      break;
    case -1:        // Joker
      goto case 12; // Make joker count as queen
    default:        // Executes for any other cardNumber
      Console.WriteLine (cardNumber);
      break;
  }
}
```

You can only switch on an expression of a type that can be statically evaluated, which restricts it to the primitive types, string types, and enum types.

At the end of each case clause, you must say explicitly where execution is to go next, with some kind of jump statement. Here are the options:

- break (jumps to the end of the switch statement)
- goto case *x* (jumps to another case clause)
- goto default (jumps to the default clause)
- Any other jump statement—namely, return, throw, continue, or goto *label*

When more than one value should execute the same code, you can list the common cases sequentially:

```
switch (cardNumber)
{
  case 13:
  case 12:
  case 11:
    Console.WriteLine ("Face card");break;
  default:
```

```
      Console.WriteLine ("Plain card");break;
  }
```

This feature of a switch statement can be pivotal in terms of producing cleaner code than multiple if-else statements.

Iteration Statements

C# enables a sequence of statements to execute repeatedly with the while, do-while, and for statements.

while and do-while loops

while loops repeatedly execute a body of code while a bool expression is true. The expression is tested *before* the body of the loop is executed. For example:

```
int i = 0;
while (i < 3)
{
  Console.Write (i);     // 012
  i++;
}
```

do-while loops differ in functionality from while loops only in that they test the expression *after* the statement block has executed. Here's the preceding example rewritten with a do-while loop:

```
int i = 0;
do
{
  Console.WriteLine(i);
  i++;
}
while (i < 3);
```

for loops

for loops are like while loops with special clauses for *initialization* and *iteration* of a loop variable. A for loop contains three clauses as follows:

```
for (initialization-clause;
     condition-clause;
     iteration-clause)
  statement-or-statement-block
```

Initialization clause
> Executes before the loop begins, used to initialize one or more variables

Condition clause
> A `bool` expression, evaluated before each loop iteration; if `false`, the loop terminates

Iteration clause
> Executes *after* each iteration of the statement block, used typically to update the loop variable

For example, the following prints the numbers 0 through 2:

```
for (int i = 0; i < 3; i++)
  Console.WriteLine (i);
```

Any of the three parts of the `for` statement may be omitted. One can implement an infinite loop such as the following (though `while(true)` may be used instead):

```
for (;;)
  Console.WriteLine("interrupt me");
```

foreach loops

The `foreach` statement iterates over each element in an enumerable object. Most of the types in C# and the .NET Framework that represent a set or list of elements are enumerable. For example, both an array and a string are enumerable. Here is an example of enumerating over the characters in a string, from the first character through to the last:

```
foreach (char c in "beer")
  Console.Write (c + " ");        // b e e r
```

We define enumerable objects in the upcoming "Enumeration and Iterators" section.

Jump Statements

The C# jump statements are break, continue, goto, return, and throw. Jump statements obey the reliability rules of try statements (see the upcoming "try Statements and Exceptions" section). First, a jump out of a try block always executes the try's finally block before reaching the target of the jump. Second, a jump cannot be made from the inside to the outside of a finally block.

The break statement

The break statement ends the execution of the body of a while loop, for loop, or switch statement:

```
int x = 0;
while (true)
{
  if (x++ > 5)
    break;      // break from the loop
}
// execution continues here after break
...
```

The continue statement

The continue statement forgoes the remaining statements in the loop and makes an early start on the next iteration. The following loop *skips* even numbers:

```
for (int i = 0; 1 < 10; i++)
{
  if ((i % 2) == 0) continue;
  Console.Write (i + " ");      // 1 3 5 7 9
}
```

The goto statement

The goto statement transfers execution to another label within the statement block. The form is as follows:

```
goto statement-label;
```

or, when used within a switch statement:

```
goto case case-constant;
```

A label statement is just a placeholder in a code block, denoted with a colon suffix. The following example iterates the numbers 1 through 5, mimicking a for loop:

```
int i = 1;
startLoop:
if (i <= 5)
{
  Console.Write (i + " ");    // 1 2 3 4 5
  i++;
  goto startLoop;
}
```

The goto case statement transfers execution to another case label in a switch block (see the earlier "The switch statement" section).

The return statement

The return statement exits the method, and must return an expression of the method's return type if the method is nonvoid:

```
static decimal AsPercentage (decimal d)
{
  decimal p = d * 100m;
  return p;                 // Return to the calling method
                            // with value
}
```

A return statement can appear anywhere in a method.

The throw statement

The throw statement throws an exception to indicate an error has occurred (see the upcoming "try Statements and Exceptions" section):

```
if (w == null)
  throw new ArgumentNullException (...);
```

Miscellaneous Statements

The lock statement is a syntactic shortcut for calling the Enter and Exit methods of the Monitor class, which provide exclusive locking functionality for multithreaded programs. (For an extensive online resource on multithreading, see *www.albahari.com/threading/*.)

The using statement provides an elegant syntax for calling Dispose on objects that implement IDisposable (see "try Statements and Exceptions" later in the book).

NOTE

C# overloads the using keyword to have independent meanings in different contexts. Specifically, the using *directive* is different from the using *statement*.

Namespaces

A *namespace* is a domain within which type names must be unique. Types are typically organized into hierarchical namespaces—both to avoid naming conflicts and to make type names easier to find. For example, the RSA type, which handles public key encryption, is defined within the following namespace:

```
System.Security.Cryptography
```

A namespace forms an integral part of a type's name. The following code calls RSA's Create method:

```
System.Security.Cryptography.RSA rsa =
  System.Security.Cryptography.RSA.Create( );
```

NOTE

Namespaces are independent of assemblies, which are units of deployment such as an *.exe* or *.dll*. Namespaces also have no impact on member visibility—public, internal, private, and so on.

The namespace keyword defines a type within a namespace. For example:

```
namespace Outer.Middle.Inner
{
  class Class1 {}
  class Class2 {}
}
```

The dots in the namespace indicate a hierarchy of nested namespaces. The following is semantically identical to the preceding example:

```
namespace Outer
{
  namespace Middle
  {
    namespace Inner
    {
      class Class1 {}
      class Class2 {}
    }
  }
}
```

You can refer to a type with is *fully qualified name*, which includes all namespaces from the outermost to the innermost. For example, we could refer to Class1 in the preceding example as Outer.Middle.Inner.Class1.

Types not defined in any namespace are said to reside in the *global namespace*. The global namespace also includes top-level namespaces, such as Outer in our example.

The using Directive

The using directive *imports* a namespace. This is a convenient way to refer to types without their fully qualified names. For example:

```
using Outer.Middle.Inner;

class Test      // Test is in the global namespace
{
```

```
    static void Main()
    {
      Class1 c;    // Don't need fully qualified name
    }
  }
```

A using directive can be nested within a namespace itself to limit the scope of the directive.

Rules Within a Namespace

Name scoping

All names present in outer namespaces are implicitly imported into inner namespaces. In this example, the names Middle and Class1 are implicitly imported into Inner:

```
namespace Outer
{
  namespace Middle
  {
    class Class1 {}

    namespace Inner
    {
      class Class2 : Class1 {}
    }
  }
}
```

If you want to refer to a type in a different branch of your namespace hierarchy, you can use a partially qualified name. In the following example, we base SalesReport on Common. ReportBase:

```
namespace MyTradingCompany
{
  namespace Common
  {
    class ReportBase {}
  }
  namespace ManagementReporting
  {
    class SalesReport : Common.ReportBase {}
  }
}
```

Name hiding

If the same type name appears in both an inner and outer namespace, the inner name wins. To refer to the outer type, you must use its fully qualified name.

NOTE

All type names are converted to fully qualified names at compile time. Intermediate Language (IL) code does not contain any unqualified or partially qualified names.

The global:: qualifier

Occasionally, a fully qualified type name may conflict with an inner name. You can force C# to use the fully qualified type name by prefixing it with `global::` as follows:

```
global::System.Text.StringBuilder sb;
```

Repeated namespaces

You can repeat a namespace declaration, as long as the type names within the namespaces don't conflict:

```
namespace Outer.Middle.Inner { class Class1 {} }
namespace Outer.Middle.Inner { class Class2 {} }
```

Aliasing Types and Namespaces

Importing a namespace can result in type-name collision. Rather than importing the whole namespace, you can import just the specific types you need, giving each type an alias. For example:

```
using PropertyInfo2 = System.Reflection.PropertyInfo;

class Program { PropertyInfo2 p; }
```

An entire namespace can be aliased, as follows:

```
using R = System.Reflection;

class Program { R.PropertyInfo p; }
```

Classes

A *class* is the most common kind of reference type. The simplest possible class declaration is as follows:

```
class YourClassName
{
}
```

A more complex class optionally has:

preceding the keyword `class`	attributes and class modifiers. The non-nested class modifiers are `public`, `internal`, `abstract`, `sealed`, `static`, `unsafe`, and `partial`
following `YourClassName`	generic type parameters, a base class, and interfaces
within the braces	class members (these are methods, properties, indexers, events, fields, constructors, operator functions, nested types, and a finalizer)

Fields

A *field* is a variable that is a member of a class or struct. For example:

```
class Octopus
{
  string name;
  public int Age = 10;
}
```

A field may have the readonly modifier to prevent it from being modified after construction. A read-only field can be assigned only in its declaration or within the enclosing type's constructor.

Field initialization

Field initialization is optional. An uninitialized field has a default value (0, \0, null, false). Field initializers run before constructors:

```
string name = "anonymous";
```

Declaring multiple fields together

For convenience, you may declare multiple fields of the same type in a comma-separated list. This is a convenient way for all the fields to share the same attributes and field modifiers. For example:

```
static readonly int legs = 8, eyes = 1;
```

Methods

A method performs an action in a series of statements. A method can receive input data from the caller by specifying parameters, and output data back to the caller by specifying a return type. A method can specify a void return type, indicating that it doesn't return any value to its caller. A method can also output data back to the caller via ref/out parameters.

A method's *signature* must be unique within the type. A method's signature comprises its name and parameter types (but not the parameter *names*, nor the return type).

Overloading methods

A type may overload methods (have many methods with the same name), as long as the signatures are different. For example, the following methods can all coexist in the same type:

```
void Foo (int x);
void Foo (double x);
void Foo (int x, float y);
void Foo (float x, int y);
```

However, the following pairs of methods cannot coexist in the same type, as the return type and the params modifier are not part of a method's signature:

```
void  Foo (int x);
float Foo (int x);             // Compile error

void  Goo (int[] x);
void  Goo (params int[] x);  // Compile error
```

Pass-by-value versus pass-by-reference

Whether a parameter is pass-by-value or pass-by-reference is also part of the signature. For example, Foo(int) can coexist with either Foo(ref int) or Foo(out int). However, Foo(ref int) and Foo(out int) cannot coexist:

```
void Foo (int x);
void Foo (ref int x);      // OK so far
void Foo (out int x);      // Compile error
```

Instance Constructors

Constructors run initialization code on a class or struct. A constructor is defined like a method, except the method name and return type are reduced to the name of the enclosing type:

```
public class Panda
{
  string name;                 // Define field
  public Panda (string n)      // Define constructor
  {
    name = n;                  // Initialization code
                               // (set up field)
  }
}
...

Panda p = new Panda ("Petey");   // Call constructor
```

Overloading constructors

A class or struct may overload constructors. To avoid code duplication, one constructor may call another, using the this keyword:

```
using System;

public class Wine
{
  public decimal Price;
  public int Year;

  public Wine (decimal price) { Price = price; }
```

```
    public Wine (decimal price, int year)
                : this (price) { Year = year; }
}
```

When one constructor calls another, the called constructor executes first.

You can pass an expression into another constructor as follows:

```
    public Wine (decimal price, DateTime year)
                : this (price, year.Year) { }
```

The expression itself cannot make use of the this reference, for example, to call an instance method. It can, however, call static methods.

Implicit parameterless constructors

For classes, the C# compiler automatically generates a parameterless constructor if and only if you do not define any constructors. However, as soon as you define at least one constructor, the parameterless constructor is no longer automatically generated.

For structs, a parameterless constructor is intrinsic to the struct; therefore, you cannot define your own. The role of a struct's implicit parameterless constructor is to initialize each field with default values.

Constructor and field initialization order

We saw previously that fields can be initialized with default values in their declaration:

```
    class Player
    {
      int shields = 50;   // Initialized first
      int health = 100;   // Initialized second
    }
```

Field initializations occur *before* the constructor is executed, and in the declaration order of the fields.

Nonpublic constructors

Constructors do not need to be public. A common reason to have a nonpublic constructor is to control instance creation via a static method call, which can be used to return an object from a pool rather than necessarily creating a new object, or return various subclasses based on input arguments.

Object Initializers (C# 3.0)

To simplify object initialization, the accessible fields or properties of an object can be initialized in a single statement directly after construction. For example, consider the following class:

```
public class Bunny
{
  public string Name;
  public bool LikesCarrots;
  public bool LikesHumans;

  public Bunny () { }
  public Bunny (string n) { Name = n; }
}
```

Using object initializers, you can instantiate Bunny objects as follows:

```
// Note parameterless constructors can omit
// empty parenthesis

Bunny b1 - new Bunny {
                       Name="Bo",
                       LikesCarrots = true,
                       LikesHumans = false
                     };

Bunny b2 = new Bunny ("Bo") {
                              LikesCarrots = true,
                              LikesHumans = false
                            };
```

this Reference

The this reference refers to the instance itself. In the following example, the Marry method uses this to set the partner's mate field:

```
public class Panda
{
  public Panda Mate;

  public void Marry (Panda partner)
  {
    Mate = partner;
    partner.Mate = this;
  }
}
```

The this reference also disambiguates a local variable or argument from a field. For example:

```
public class Test
{
  string name;
  public Test (string name) { this.name = name; }
}
```

The this reference is valid only within nonstatic members of a class or struct.

Properties

Properties look like fields from the outside but act like methods on the inside. For example, you can't tell by looking at the following code whether CurrentPrice is a field or a property:

```
Stock msft = new Stock();
msft.CurrentPrice = 30;
msft.CurrentPrice -= 3;
Console.WriteLine (msft.CurrentPrice);
```

A property is declared like a field, but with a get/set block added. Here's how to implement CurrentPrice as a property:

```
public class Stock
{
  decimal currentPrice;  // The private "backing" field
```

```
public decimal CurrentPrice      // The public property
{
    get { return currentPrice; }
    set { currentPrice = value; }
}
}
```

get and set denote property *accessors*. The get accessor runs when the property is read. It must return a value of the property's type. The set accessor is run when the property is assigned. It has an implicit parameter named value of the property's type that you typically assign to a private field (in this case, currentPrice).

Although properties are accessed in the same way as fields, they differ in that they give the implementer complete control over getting and setting its value. This control enables the implementer to choose whatever internal representation is needed, without exposing the internal details to the user of the property. In this example, the set method could throw an exception if value was outside a valid range of values.

NOTE

Throughout this book, we use public fields extensively to keep the examples free of distraction. In a real application, you would typically favor public properties over public fields to promote encapsulation.

Read-only and calculated properties

A property is read-only if it specifies only a get accessor, and it is write-only if it specifies only a set accessor. Write-only properties are rarely used.

A property typically has a dedicated backing field to store the underlying data. However, a property can also be computed from other data, for example:

```
decimal currentPrice, sharesOwned;
```

```
public decimal Worth
{
  get { return currentPrice * sharesOwned; }
}
```

Automatic properties (C# 3.0)

The most common implementation for a property is a getter and/or setter that simply reads and writes to a private field of the same type as the property. An *automatic property* declaration instructs the compiler to provide this implementation. We can redeclare the first example in this section as follows:

```
public class Stock
{
  ...
  public decimal CurrentPrice { get; set; }
}
```

The compiler automatically generates a private backing field of a compiler-generated name that cannot be referred to. The set accessor can be marked private if you want to expose the property as read-only to other types.

get and set accessibility

The get and set accessors are permitted to have different access levels. The typical use case is to have a public property with an internal or private access modifier on the setter:

```
private decimal x;
public decimal X
{
  get          { return x; }
  internal set { x = value; }
}
```

Indexers

Indexers provide a natural syntax for accessing elements in a class or struct that encapsulates a list or dictionary of values. Indexers are similar to properties, but are accessed via an index argument rather than a property name. The string class has an indexer that lets you access each of its char values via an int index:

```
string s = "hello";
Console.WriteLine (s[0]); // 'h'
Console.WriteLine (s[3]); // 'l'
```

The syntax for using indexers is like that of using arrays, when the index is an integer type.

NOTE

Indexers allow the same modifiers as properties (see the previous section on property modifiers).

Implementing an indexer

To write an indexer, define a property called this, specifying the arguments in square brackets. For instance:

```
class Sentence
{
  string[] words = "The quick brown fox".Split( );

  public string this [int wordNum]      // indexer
  {
    get { return words [wordNum];  }
    set { words [wordNum] = value; }
  }
}
```

Here's how we could use this indexer:

```
Sentence s = new Sentence( );
Console.WriteLine (s[3]);         // fox
s[3] = "kangaroo";
Console.WriteLine (s[3]);         // kangaroo
```

A type may declare multiple indexers, each with parameters of different types. An indexer can also take more than one parameter:

```
public string this [int arg1, string arg2]
{
  get { ... }  set { ... }
}
```

Constants

A *constant* is a field whose value can never change. A constant is evaluated statically at compile time and its value is literally substituted by the compiler whenever used, rather like a macro in C++. A constant can be any of the built-in numeric types, bool, char, string, or an enum type.

A constant is declared with the const keyword and must be initialized with a value. For example:

```
public class Test
{
  public const string Message = "Hello World";
}
```

A constant is much more restrictive than a static readonly field—both in the types you can use, and in field initialization semantics. A constant also differs from a static readonly field in that the evaluation of the constant occurs at compile time. For example:

```
public static double Circumference (double radius)
{
  return 2 * System.Math.PI * radius;
}
```

is compiled to:

```
public static double Circumference (double radius)
{
  return 6.2831853071795862 * radius;
}
```

It makes sense for PI to be a constant, as it can never change. In contrast, a static readonly field can have a different value per application.

Constants can also be declared local to a method. For example:

```
static void Main()
{
  const double twoPI  = 2 * System.Math.PI;
  ...
}
```

Static Constructors

A *static constructor* executes once per *type*—rather than once per *instance*. A static constructor executes before any instances of the type are created, and before any other static members are accessed. A type can define only one static constructor, and it must be parameterless and have the same name as the type:

```
class Test
{
  static Test()
  {
    Console.WriteLine ("Type Initialized");
  }
}
```

The only modifiers allowed by static constructors are unsafe and extern.

Any static field assignments are performed *before* the static constructor is called, in the declaration order in which the fields appear.

Nondeterminism of static constructors

A static constructor is always invoked indirectly by the runtime—it cannot be called explicitly. The runtime guarantees to invoke a type's static constructor *at some point* prior to the type being used; it doesn't commit, though, to exactly *when*. For example, a subclass's static constructor can execute before or after that of its base class. The runtime may also choose to invoke static constructors *unnecessarily* early, from a programmer's perspective.

Static Classes

A class can be marked static, indicating that it must be comprised solely of static members and cannot be subclassed. The System.Console and System.Math classes are good examples of static classes.

Finalizers

Finalizers are class-only methods that execute just before the garbage collector reclaims the memory for an unreferenced object. The syntax for a finalizer is the name of the class prefixed with the ~ symbol:

```
class Class1
{
  ~Class1() { ... }
}
```

This is actually C# syntax for overriding Object's Finalize method, and it is expanded by the compiler into the following method declaration:

```
protected override void Finalize()
{
  ...
  base.Finalize();
}
```

We describe the implications of finalizers in detail in Chapter 12 of *C# 3.0 in a Nutshell* (O'Reilly).

Partial Types and Methods

Partial types allow a type definition to be split, typically across multiple files. A common scenario is for a partial class to be auto-generated from some other source (e.g., an XSD), and for that class to be augmented with additional hand-authored methods. For example:

```
// PaymentFormGen.cs - auto-generated
partial class PaymentForm { ... }

// PaymentForm.cs - hand-authored
partial class PaymentForm { ... }
```

Each participant must have the partial declaration; the following is illegal:

```
partial class PaymentForm { }
class PaymentForm { }
```

Participants cannot have conflicting members. A constructor with the same arguments, for instance, cannot be repeated. Partial types are resolved entirely by the compiler, which means that each participant must be available at compile time and must reside in the same assembly.

You can specify a base class on one or more partial participants—as long as there's no disagreement in the base class name. Base classes are used for inheritance (see the upcoming "Inheritance" section).

Partial methods (C# 3.0)

A partial type may contain *partial methods*. Partial methods let an auto-generated partial type provide customizable hooks for manual authoring. For example:

```
partial class PaymentForm    // In auto-generated file
{
  ...
  partial void ValidatePayment (decimal amount);
}

partial class PaymentForm    // In hand-authored file
{
  ...
  partial void ValidatePayment (decimal amount)
  {
    if (amount > 100)
      throw new ArgumentException ("Too expensive");
  }
}
```

A partial method consists of two parts: a definition and an implementation. The definition is typically written by a code generator, and the implementation is typically manually authored. If an implementation is not provided, the definition of the partial method is compiled away. This allows auto-generated code to be liberal in providing hooks, without having to worry about code bloat. Partial methods must be void and are implicitly private.

Inheritance

A class can *inherit* from another class to extend or customize the original class. Inheriting from a class lets you reuse the functionality in that class instead of building it from scratch. A class can inherit from only a single class, but can itself be inherited by many classes, thus forming a class hierarchy. In this example, we start by defining a class called Asset:

```
public class Asset
{
  public string Name;
}
```

Next, we define classes called Stock and House, which will inherit from Asset. Stock and House get everything an Asset has, plus any additional members that they define:

```
public class Stock : Asset     // inherits from Asset
{
  public long SharesOwned;
}

public class House : Asset     // inherits from Asset
{
  public decimal Mortgage;
}
```

Here's how we can use these classes:

```
Stock msft = new Stock { Name="MSFT",
                         SharesOwned=1000 };

Console.WriteLine (msft.Name);        // MSFT
Console.WriteLine (msft.SharesOwned); // 1000

House mansion = new House { Name="Mansion",
                            Mortgage=250000 };

Console.WriteLine (mansion.Name);     // Mansion
Console.WriteLine (mansion.Mortgage); // 250000
```

The *subclasses* Stock and House inherit the Name property from the *base class* Asset.

A subclass is also called a *derived class*. A base class is also called a *superclass*.

Polymorphism

References are *polymorphic*, which means a reference to a base class can refer to an instance of a subclass. For instance, consider the following method:

```
public static void Display (Asset asset)
{
  System.Console.WriteLine (asset.Name);
}
```

This method can display both a Stock and a House because they are both Assets:

```
Stock msft    = new Stock ... ;
House mansion = new House ... ;

Display (msft);
Display (mansion);
```

Polymorphism works on the basis that subclasses (Stock and House) have all the features of their base class (Asset). The converse, however, is not true. If Display was modified to accept a House, you could not pass in an Asset.

Casting

An object reference can be:

- Implicitly *upcast* to a base class reference
- Explicitly *downcast* to a subclass reference

Casting only affects *references*; the object itself is not converted or altered. An upcast always succeeds; a downcast succeeds only if the object is suitably typed.

Upcasting

An upcast operation creates a base class reference from a subclass reference. For example:

```
Stock msft = new Stock ...;
Asset a = msft;                    // upcast
```

After the upcast, variable a still references the same Stock object as variable msft. The object being referenced is not itself altered or converted:

```
Console.WriteLine (a == msft);     // True
```

Although a and msft refer to the identical object, a has a more restrictive view on that object:

```
Console.WriteLine (a.Name);        // OK
Console.WriteLine (a.SharesOwned); // Error
```

The last line generates a compile-time error because the reference a is of type Asset, even though it refers to an object of type Stock. To get to its SharedOwned field, you must downcast the Asset to a Stock.

Downcasting

A downcast operation creates a subclass reference from a base class reference. For example:

```
Stock msft = new Stock();
Asset a = msft;                     // upcast
Stock s = (Stock)a;                 // downcast
Console.WriteLine (s.SharesOwned);  // <No error>
Console.WriteLine (s == a);         // true
Console.WriteLine (s == msft);      // true
```

As with an upcast, only references are affected—not the underlying object. A downcast requires an explicit cast because it can potentially fail at runtime:

```
House h = new House();
Asset a = h;           // Upcast always succeeds
Stock s = (Stock)a;    // Downcast fails: a is not a Stock
```

If a downcast fails, an `InvalidCastException` is thrown. This is an example of *dynamic type checking* (we will elaborate on this concept in the upcoming "Static and Dynamic Type Checking" section).

The as operator

The as operator performs a downcast that evaluates to `null` if the downcast fails (rather than throwing an exception):

```
Asset a = new Asset();
Stock s = a as Stock;        // s is null
```

The is operator

The is operator tests whether a downcast would succeed; in other words, whether an object derives from a specified class (or implements an interface). It is often used to test before downcasting:

```
if (a is Stock)
  Console.WriteLine (((Stock)a).SharesOwned);
```

Virtual Function Members

A function marked as virtual can be *overridden* by subclasses wanting to provide a specialized implementation. Methods, properties, indexers, and events can all be declared virtual:

```
public class Asset
{
  public string Name;

  public virtual decimal Liability
    { get { return 0; } }
}
```

A subclass overrides a virtual method by applying the override modifier:

```
public class Stock : Asset { public long SharesOwned; }
```

```
public class House : Asset
{
  public decimal Mortgage;

  public override decimal Liability
    { get { return Mortgage; } }
}
```

By default, the Liability of an Asset is 0. A Stock does not
need to specialize this behavior. However, the House special-
izes the Liability property to return the value of the Mortgage:

```
House mansion = new House { Name="Mansion",
                            Mortgage=250000 };
Asset a = mansion;
decimal d2 = mansion.Liability;      // 250000
```

The signatures, return types, and accessibility of the virtual
and overridden methods must be identical. An overridden
method can call its base class implementation via the base
keyword (we will cover this shortly, in the upcoming "The
base Keyword" section).

Abstract Classes and Abstract Members

A class declared as *abstract* can never be instantiated.
Instead, only its concrete *subclasses* can be instantiated.

Abstract classes are able to define *abstract members*, which are
like virtual members, except they don't provide a default
implementation. That implementation must be provided by
the subclass, unless that subclass is also declared abstract:

```
public abstract class Asset
{
  // Note empty implementation
  public abstract decimal NetValue { get; }
}

public class Stock : Asset
{
  public long SharesOwned;
  public decimal CurrentPrice;
```

```
  // Override like a virtual method.
  public override decimal NetValue
  {
    get { return CurrentPrice * SharesOwned; }
  }
}
```

Hiding Inherited Members

A base class and a subclass may define identical members.
For example:

```
public class A     { public int Counter = 1; }
public class B : A { public int Counter = 2; }
```

The Counter field in class B is said to *hide* the Counter field in
class A. Usually, this happens accidentally, when a member is
added to the base type *after* an identical member was added
to the subtype. For this reason, the compiler generates a
warning, and then resolves the ambiguity as follows:

* References to A (at compile time) bind to A.Counter.
* References to B (at compile time) bind to B.Counter.

Occasionally, you want to hide a member deliberately, in
which case, you can apply the new modifier to the member in
the subclass. The new modifier *does nothing more than suppress the compiler warning that would otherwise result*:

```
public class A     { public     int Counter = 1; }
public class B : A { public new int Counter = 2; }
```

The new modifier communicates your intent to the compiler—and other programmers—that the duplicate member
is not an accident.

NOTE

C# overloads the new keyword to have independent
meanings in different contexts. Specifically, the new *operator* is different from the new *member* modifier.

Sealing Functions and Classes

An overridden function member may *seal* its implementation with the sealed keyword to prevent it from being overridden by further subclasses. In our earlier virtual function member example, we could have sealed House's implementation of Liability, preventing a class that derives from House from overriding Liability, as follows:

```
public sealed override decimal Liability
  { get { return Mortgage; } }
```

You can also seal the class itself, implicitly sealing all the virtual functions, by applying the sealed modifier to the class itself. Sealing a class is more common than sealing a function member.

The base Keyword

The base keyword is similar to the this keyword. It serves two essential purposes:

- Accessing an overridden function member from the subclass
- Calling a base class constructor (see the next section)

In this example, House uses the base keyword to access Asset's implementation of Liability:

```
public class House : Asset
{
  ...
  public override decimal Liability
  {
    get { return base.Liability + Mortgage; }
  }
}
```

The same approach works if Liability is *hidden* rather than *overridden*. (You can also access hidden members by casting to the base class before invoking the function.)

Constructors and Inheritance

A subclass must declare its own constructors. For example, if we define Subclass as follows:

```
public class Baseclass
{
  public int X;
  public Baseclass ()
  public Baseclass (int x) { this.X = x; }
}

public class Subclass : Baseclass { }
```

the following is illegal:

```
Subclass s = new Subclass (123);
```

Subclass must hence redeclare any constructors it wants to expose. In doing so, however, it can call any of the base class's constructors with the base keyword:

```
public class Subclass : Baseclass
{
  public Subclass (int x) : base (x) { }
}
```

The base keyword works rather like the this keyword, except that it calls a constructor in the base class.

Base class constructors always execute first; this ensures that *base* initialization occurs before *specialized* initialization.

Implicit calling of the parameterless base class constructor

If a constructor in a subclass omits the base keyword, the base type's *parameterless* constructor is implicitly called. If the base class has no parameterless constructor, subclasses are forced to use the base keyword in their constructors.

Constructor and field initialization order

When an object is instantiated, initialization takes place in the following order:

From subclass to base class:

- Fields are initialized.
- Constructor arguments are evaluated.

From base class to subclass:

- Constructor bodies execute.

Overloading and Resolution

Inheritance has an interesting impact on method overloading. Consider the following two overloads:

```
static void Foo (Asset a) { }
static void Foo (House h) { }
```

When an overload is called, the most specific type has precedence:

```
House h = new House (...);
Foo (h);                   // calls Foo (House)
```

The particular overload to call is determined statically (at compile time) rather than dynamically (at runtime). The following code calls Foo(Asset), even though the runtime type of a is House:

```
Asset a = new House (...);
Foo (a);                   // calls Foo (Asset)
```

The object Type

object (System.Object) is the ultimate base class for all types. Any type can be upcast to object.

To illustrate how this is useful, consider a general-purpose stack. A stack is a data structure based on the principle of LIFO—"Last in, First out." A stack has two operations: *push* an object on the stack, and *pop* an object off the stack.

Here is a simple implementation that can hold up to 10 objects:

```
public class Stack
{
  int position;
  object[] data = new object[10];

  public void Push (object obj)
    { data[position++] = obj;  }

  public object Pop()
    { return data[--position]; }
}
```

Because Stack works with the object type, we can Push and Pop instances of *any type* to and from the Stack:

```
Stack stack = new Stack();
stack.Push ("sausage");

// Explicit cast is needed because we're downcasting:
string s = (string) stack.Pop();

Console.WriteLine (s);              // sausage
```

object is a reference type, by virtue of being a class. Despite this, value types, such as int, can also be cast to and from object, and so be added to our stack. This feature of C# is called *type unification*:

```
stack.Push (3);
int three = (int) stack.Pop();
```

When you cast between a value type and object, the CLR must perform some special work to bridge the difference in semantics between value and reference types. This process is called *boxing* and *unboxing*.

Boxing and Unboxing

Boxing is the act of casting a value type instance to a reference type instance. The reference type may be either the object class, or an interface (which we will visit later). In this example, we *box* an int into an object:

```
int x = 9;
object obj = x;          // box the int
```

Unboxing reverses the operation, by casting the object back to the original value type:

```
int y = (int)obj;        // unbox the int
```

Unboxing requires an explicit cast. The runtime checks that the stated value type (exactly) matches the actual object type, and throws an `InvalidCastException` if the check fails. For instance, the following throws an exception because `long` does not exactly match `int`:

```
object obj = 9;          // 9 is inferred to be of type int
long x = (long) obj;     // InvalidCastException
```

The following succeeds, however:

```
object obj = 9;
long x = (int) obj;
```

as does this:

```
object obj = 3.5;             // inferred type is double
int x = (int) (double) obj;   // x is now 3
```

In the last example, (int) performs a *conversion*; (double) performs an *unboxing*.

Copying semantics of boxing and unboxing

Boxing copies the value type instance into the new object, and unboxing copies the contents of the object back into a value type instance.

Static and Dynamic Type Checking

C# checks types both *statically* and *dynamically*.

Static type checking occurs at *compile time*. Static type checking enables the compiler to verify the correctness of your program without running it. The following code will fail because the compiler enforces static typing:

```
int x = "5";
```

Dynamic type checking occurs at *runtime*. Whenever an unboxing or downcast occurs, the runtime checks the type dynamically. For example:

```
object y = "5";
int z = (int)y;    // Runtime error, downcast failed
```

Dynamic type checking is possible because each object on the heap internally stores a little type token. This token can be retrieved by calling the GetType method of object.

Object Member Listing

Here are all the members of object:

```
public class Object
{
  public Object();
  public extern Type GetType();
  public virtual bool Equals (object obj);
  public static bool Equals (object objA, object objB);
  public static bool ReferenceEquals (object objA,
                                      object objB);
  public virtual int GetHashCode();
  public virtual string ToString();
  protected override void Finalize();
  protected extern object MemberwiseClone();
}
```

GetType( ) and typeof

All types in C# are represented at runtime with an instance of System.Type. There are two basic ways to get a System.Type object:

- Call GetType on the instance.
- Use the typeof operator on a type name.

GetType is evaluated dynamically at runtime; typeof is evaluated statically at compile time.

System.Type has properties for such things as the type's name, assembly, base type, and so on. For example:

```
int x = 3;

Console.Write (x.GetType( ).Name);          // Int32
Console.Write (typeof(int).Name);           // Int32
Console.Write (x.GetType( ).FullName);   // System.Int32
Console.Write (x.GetType( ) == typeof(int));   // True
```

System.Type also has methods that act as a gateway to the runtime's reflection model. For detailed information, see Chapter 17 of *C# 3.0 in a Nutshell*.

Equals, ReferenceEquals, and GetHashCode

The Equals method is similar to the == operator, except that Equals is virtual, whereas == is static. The following example illustrates the difference:

```
object x = 3;
object y = 3;
Console.WriteLine (x == y);        // False
Console.WriteLine (x.Equals (y));  // True
```

Because x and y have been cast to the object type, the compiler statically binds to object's == operator, which uses *reference-type* semantics to compare two instances. (And because x and y are boxed, they are represented in separate memory locations, and so are unequal.) The virtual Equals method, however, defers to the Int32 type's Equals method, which uses *value-type* semantics in comparing two values.

The static object.Equals method simply calls the virtual Equals method—after checking that the arguments are not null.

```
object x = null;
object y = 3;
bool error = x.Equals (y);     // NullReferenceException
bool ok = object.Equals (x, y);
```

ReferenceEquals forces a reference-type equality comparison (this is occasionally useful on reference types where the == operator has been overloaded to do otherwise).

GetHashCode emits a hash code when the type is used in a hashtable-based dictionary, namely System.Collections. Generic.Dictionary and System.Collections.Hashtable.

To customize a type's equality semantics, you must at a minimum override Equals and GetHashCode. You would also usually overload the == and != operators. For an example on how to do both, see the upcoming "Operator Overloading" section.

The ToString Method

The ToString method returns the default textual representation of a type instance. The ToString method is overridden by all built-in types. Here is an example of using the int type's ToString method:

```
int x = 1;
string s = x.ToString( );    // s is "1"
```

You can override the ToString method on custom types as follows:

```
public class Panda
{
  public string Name;
  public override string ToString( ) { return Name; }
}
...

Panda p = new Panda { Name = "Petey" };
Console.WriteLine (p);   // Petey
```

NOTE

When you call an overridden object member such as ToString directly on a value type, boxing doesn't occur—boxing occurs only when you cast.

Structs

A *struct* is similar to a class, with the following key differences:

- A struct is a value type, whereas a class is a reference type.
- A struct does not support inheritance (other than implicitly deriving from object).

A struct can have all the members a class can, except:

- A parameterless constructor
- A finalizer
- Virtual members

A struct is used instead of a class when value type semantics are desirable. Good examples of structs are numeric types, where it is more natural for assignment to copy a value rather than a reference. Because a struct is a value type, each instance does not require instantiation of an object on the heap. This can be important when creating many instances of a type, for example, with an array.

Struct Construction Semantics

The construction semantics of a struct are as follows:

- A parameterless constructor implicitly exists, which you can't override. This performs a bitwise-zeroing of its fields.
- When you define a struct constructor, you must explicitly assign every field.
- You can't have field initializers in a struct.

Here is an example of declaring and calling struct constructors:

```
public struct Point
{
  int x, y;
  public Point (int x, int y) {this.x = x; this.y = y;}
}

...
```

```
Point p1 = new Point ();     // p1.x and p1.y will be 0
Point p2 = new Point (1, 1); // p1.x and p1.y will be 1
```

The next example generates three compile-time errors:

```
public struct Point
{
  int x = 1;          // Illegal, cannot initialize field
  int y;
  public Point() {} // Illegal, cannot have
                     // parameterless constructor

  public Point(int x) {this.x = x;}  // illegal, must
                                     // assign field y
}
```

Changing struct to class makes this example legal.

Access Modifiers

To promote encapsulation, a type or type member may limit its *accessibility* to other types and other assemblies by adding one of five *access modifiers* to the declaration:

public
> Fully accessible. The implicit accessibility for members of an enum or interface.

internal
> Accessible only within containing assembly or friend assemblies. The default accessibility for nonnested types.

private
> Visible only within containing type. The default accessibility members of a class or struct.

protected
> Visible only within containing type or subclasses.

protected internal
> The *union* of protected and internal accessibility. (This is *less* restrictive than protected or internal alone.)

Examples

Class2 is accessible from outside its assembly; Class1 is not:

```
class Class1        { }  // Class1 is internal (default)
public class Class2 { }
```

ClassB exposes field x to other types in the same assembly; ClassA does not:

```
class ClassA { int x;        }  // x is private
                                // (default)
class ClassB { internal int x; }
```

Functions within Subclass can call Bar but not Foo:

```
class BaseClass
{
  void Foo()           { }  // Foo is private (default)
  protected void Bar() { }
}

class Subclass : BaseClass
{
    void Test1() { Foo(); }  // Error: cannot access Foo
    void Test2() { Bar(); }  // OK
}
```

Accessibility Capping

A type caps the accessibility of its declared members. The most common example of capping is when you have an internal type with public members. For example:

```
class C { public void Foo() {} }
```

C's (default) internal accessibility caps Foo's accessibility, effectively making Foo internal. The reason Foo would be marked public is to make for easier refactoring, should C later be changed to public.

Restrictions on Access Modifiers

When overriding a base class function, accessibility must be identical on the overridden function.

The compiler also prevents any inconsistent use of access modifiers. For example, a subclass itself can be less accessible than a base class, but not more accessible:

```
internal class A   { }
public class B : A { }       // Error
```

Interfaces

An interface is similar to a class, but it provides a specification rather than an implementation for its members. An interface is special in the following ways:

- A class can implement *multiple* interfaces. In contrast, a class can inherit from only a *single* class.
- Interface members are *all implicitly abstract*. In contrast, a class can provide both abstract members and concrete members with implementations.
- Structs can implement interfaces. In contrast, a struct cannot inherit from a class.

An interface declaration is like a class declaration, but it provides no implementation for its members, as all its members are implicitly abstract. These members will be implemented by the classes and structs that implement the interface. An interface can contain only methods, properties, events, and indexers, which noncoincidentally are precisely the members of a class that can be abstract.

Here is a slightly simplified version of the IEnumerator interface, defined in System.Collections:

```
public interface IEnumerator
{
  bool MoveNext();
  object Current {get;}
}
```

Interface members have the same accessibility as the interface type, and they cannot declare an access modifier.

Implementing an interface means providing a `public` implementation for all its members:

```
internal class Countdown : IEnumerator
{
  int count = 11;
  public bool MoveNext()  { return count-- > 0 ; }
  public object Current   { get { return count; } }
}
```

You can implicitly cast an object to any interface that it implements. For example:

```
IEnumerator e = new Countdown( );
while (e.MoveNext( ))
  Console.Write (e.Current);        // 109876543210
```

NOTE

Even though Countdown is an internal class, its members that implement IEnumerator can be called publicly by casting an instance of Countdown to IEnumerator. If IEnumerator was itself internal instead of public, this wouldn't be possible.

Extending an Interface

Interfaces may derive from other interfaces. For instance:

```
public interface IUndoable            { void Undo( ); }
public interface IRedoable : IUndoable { void Redo( ); }
```

IRedoable inherits all the members of IUndoable.

Explicit Interface Implementation

Implementing multiple interfaces can sometimes result in a collision between member signatures. You can resolve such collisions by *explicitly implementing* an interface member. Consider the following example:

```
interface I1 { void Foo(); }
interface I2 { int Foo(); }

public class Widget : I1, I2
{
  public void Foo()
  {
    Console.WriteLine
      ("Widget's implementation of I1.Foo");
  }

  int I2.Foo()
  {
    Console.WriteLine
      ("Widget's implementation of I2.Foo");
    return 42;
  }
}
```

Because both I1 and I2 have conflicting Foo signatures, Widget explicitly implements I2's Foo method. This lets the two methods coexist in one class. The only way to call an explicitly implemented member is to cast to its interface:

```
Widget w = new Widget();
w.Foo();              // Widget's implementation of I1.Foo
((I1)w).Foo();        // Widget's implementation of I1.Foo
((I2)w).Foo();        // Widget's implementation of I2.Foo
```

Another reason to explicitly implement interface members is to hide members that are highly specialized and distracting to a type's normal use case. For example, a type that implements ISerializable would typically want to avoid flaunting its ISerializable members unless explicitly cast to that interface.

Implementing Interface Members Virtually

An implicitly implemented interface member is, by default, sealed. It must be marked virtual or abstract in the base class to be overridden. For example:

```
public interface IUndoable { void Undo( ); }

public class TextBox : IUndoable
{
  public virtual void Undo( )
  {
    Console.WriteLine ("TextBox.Undo");
  }
}

public class RichTextBox : TextBox
{
  public override void Undo( )
  {
    Console.WriteLine ("RichTextBox.Undo");
  }
}
```

Calling the interface member through either the base class or the interface calls the subclass's implementation:

```
RichTextBox r = new RichTextBox( );
r.Undo( );                          // RichTextBox.Undo
((IUndoable)r).Undo( );             // RichTextBox.Undo
((TextBox)r).Undo( );               // RichTextBox.Undo
```

An explicitly implemented interface member cannot be marked virtual, nor can it be overridden in the usual manner. It can, however, be *reimplemented*.

Reimplementing an Interface in a Subclass

A subclass can reimplement any interface member already implemented by a base class. Reimplementation hijacks a member implementation (when called through the interface) and works whether or not the member is virtual in the base class. It also works whether a member is implemented implicitly or explicitly—although it works best in the latter case, as we will demonstrate.

In the following example, TextBox explicitly implements IUndo.Undo, so it cannot be marked as virtual. To "override" it, RichTextBox must reimplement IUndo's Undo method:

```
public interface IUndoable { void Undo(); }

public class TextBox : IUndoable
{
  void IUndoable.Undo()
    { Console.WriteLine ("TextBox.Undo"); }
}

public class RichTextBox : TextBox, IUndoable
{
  public new void Undo()
    { Console.WriteLine ("RichTextBox.Undo"); }
}
```

Calling the reimplemented member through the interface
calls the subclass's implementation:

```
RichTextBox r = new RichTextBox();
r.Undo();                   // RichTextBox.Undo    Case 1
((IUndoable)r).Undo();      // RichTextBox.Undo    Case 2
```

Assuming the same RichTextBox definition, suppose now that
TextBox implemented Undo *implicitly*:

```
public class TextBox : IUndoable
{
  public void Undo()
    { Console.WriteLine ("TextBox.Undo"); }
}
```

This would give us another way to call Undo, which would
"break" the system, as shown in Case 3:

```
RichTextBox r = new RichTextBox();
r.Undo();                   // RichTextBox.Undo    Case 1
((IUndoable)r).Undo();      // RichTextBox.Undo    Case 2
((TextBox)r).Undo();        // TextBox.Undo        Case 3
```

Case 3 demonstrates that reimplementation hijacking is
effective only when a member is called through the interface,
and not through the base class. This is usually undesirable as
it can mean inconsistent semantics, making reimplementation most appropriate for overriding *explicitly* implemented
interface members.

Enums

An *enum* is a special value type that lets you specify a group of named numeric constants. For example:

```
public enum BorderSide { Left, Right, Top, Bottom }
```

We can use this enum type as follows:

```
BorderSide topSide = BorderSide.Top;
bool isTop = (topSide == BorderSide.Top);   // true
```

Each enum member has an underlying integral value. By default:

- Underlying values are of type int.
- The constants 0, 1, 2... are automatically assigned in the declaration order of the enum members.

You may specify an alternative integral type, as follows:

```
public enum BorderSide : byte
  { Left, Right, Top, Bottom }
```

You may also specify an explicit underlying value for each enum member:

```
public enum BorderSide : byte
  { Left=1, Right=2, Top=10, Bottom=11 }
```

NOTE

The compiler also lets you explicitly assign *some* of the enum members. The unassigned enum members keep incrementing from the last explicit value. The preceding example is equivalent to:

```
public enum BorderSide : byte
{ Left=1, Right, Top=10, Bottom }
```

Enum Conversions

You can convert an enum instance to and from its underlying integral value with an explicit cast:

```
int i = (int) BorderSide.Left;
BorderSide side = (BorderSide) i;
bool horizontal = (int) side <= 2;
```

You can also explicitly cast one enum type to another. Suppose HorizontalAlignment is defined as follows:

```
public enum HorizontalAlignment
{
  Left = BorderSide.Left,
  Right = BorderSide.Right,
  Center
}
```

A translation between the enum types uses the underlying integral values:

```
HorizontalAlignment h = (HorizontalAlignment)
  BorderSide.Right;

// same as:

HorizontalAlignment h = (HorizontalAlignment) (int)
  BorderSide.Right;
```

The numeric literal 0 is treated specially by the compiler in an enum expression and does not require an explicit cast:

```
BorderSide b = 0;    // no cast required
if (b == 0) ...
```

There are two reasons for the special treatment of 0:

- The first member of an enum is often used as the "default" value.
- For *combined enum* types, 0 means "no flags."

Flags Enumerations

You can combine enum members. To prevent ambiguities, members of a combinable enum require explicitly assigned values, typically in powers of two. For example:

```
[Flags]
public enum BorderSides
  { Left=1, Right=2, Top=4, Bottom=8 }
```

To work with combined enum values, use bitwise operators, such as | and &. These operate on the underlying integral values:

```
BorderSides leftRight =
  BorderSides.Left | BorderSides.Right;

if ((leftRight & BorderSides.Left) != 0)
  System.Console.WriteLine ("Includes Left");

// OUTPUT: "Includes Left"

string formatted = leftRight.ToString();
// formatted is "Left, Right"

BorderSides s = BorderSides.Left;
s |= BorderSides.Right;
Console.WriteLine (s == leftRight);   // True

s ^= BorderSides.Right;    // Toggles BorderSides.Right
Console.WriteLine (s);     // Left
```

By convention, the Flags attribute should always be applied to an enum type when its members are combinable. If you declare such an enum without the Flags attribute, you can still combine members, but calling ToString on an enum instance will emit a number rather than a series of names.

By convention, a combinable enum type is given a plural rather than singular name.

For convenience, you can include combination members within an enum declaration itself:

```
[Flags] public enum BorderSides
{
  Left=1, Right=2, Top=4, Bottom=8,
  LeftRight = Left | Right,
  TopBottom = Top  | Bottom,
  All       = LeftRight | TopBottom
}
```

Enum Operators

The operators that work with enums are:

```
=    ==    !=    <    >    <=    >=    +    -    ^    &    |    ~
+=    -=    ++    --    sizeof
```

The bitwise, arithmetic, and comparison operators return the result of processing the underlying integral values. Addition and subtraction are permitted between an enum and an integral type but not between two enums.

Nested Types

A *nested type* is declared within the scope of another type. For example:

```
public class TopLevel
{
  public class Nested { }              // Nested class
  public enum Color { Red, Blue, Tan } // Nested enum
}
```

A nested type has the following features:

- It can access the enclosing type's private members and everything else the enclosing type can access.
- It can be declared with the full range of access modifiers, rather than just public and internal.
- The default visibility for a nested type is private rather than internal.
- Accessing a nested type from outside the enclosing type requires qualification with the enclosing type's name (like when accessing static members).

For example, to access Color.Red from outside our TopLevel class, we'd have to do this:

```
TopLevel.Color color = TopLevel.Color.Red;
```

All types can be nested; however, only classes and structs can *nest*. Nested types are used heavily by the compiler itself, when it generates private classes that capture state for constructs such as iterators and anonymous methods.

If the sole reason for using a nested type is to avoid clut-
tering a namespace with too many types, consider using a
nested namespace instead. A nested type should be used
because of its stronger access control restrictions, or
when the nested class must access private members of the
containing class.

Generics

C# has two separate mechanisms for writing code that is
reusable across different types: inheritance and *generics*.
Whereas inheritance expresses reusability with a base type,
generics express reusability with a "template" that contains
"placeholder" types. Generics, when compared to inheritance, can *increase type safety* and *reduce casting and boxing*.

Generic Types

A *generic type* declares *generic parameters*—placeholder
types to be filled in by the consumer of the generic type, who
will supply the *generic arguments*. Here is a generic type
Stack<T>, designed to stack instances of type T. Stack<T>
declares a single generic parameter T:

```
public class Stack<T>
{
  int position;
  T[] data = new T[100];
  public void Push (T obj) { data[position++] = obj;  }
  public T Pop()           { return data[--position]; }
}
```

We can use Stack<T> as follows:

```
Stack<int> stack = new Stack<int>();
stack.Push(5);
stack.Push(10);
int x = stack.Pop();      // x is 10
int y = stack.Pop();      // y is 5
```

Stack<int> fills in the generic parameter T with the generic argument int, implicitly creating a type on the fly (the synthesis occurs at runtime). Stack<int> effectively has the following definition (substitutions appear in bold, with the class name hashed out to avoid confusion):

```
public class ###
{
  int position;
  int[] data;
  public void Push (int obj) { data[position++] = obj; }
  public int Pop()           { return data[--position];}
}
```

Technically, we say that Stack<T> is an *open type*, whereas Stack<int> is a *closed type*. You can only instantiate a closed type, because all the placeholder types must be filled in.

Why Generics Exist

Generics exist to write code that is reusable across different types. Suppose we needed a stack of integers, but we didn't have generic types. One solution would be to hardcode a separate version of the class for every required element type (e.g., IntStack, StringStack, etc.) Clearly, this would cause considerable code duplication. Another solution would be to write a stack that is generalized by using object as the element type:

```
public class ObjectStack
{
  int position;
  object[] data = new object[10];
  public void Push (object obj){data[position++] = obj;}
  public object Pop()          { return data[--position];}
}
```

An ObjectStack, however, wouldn't work as well as a hardcoded IntStack for specifically stacking integers. Specifically, an ObjectStack would require boxing and downcasting that could not be checked at compile time:

```
// Suppose we just want to store integers here:
ObjectStack stack = new ObjectStack( );

stack.Push ("s");          // Wrong type, but no error!
int i = (int)stack.Pop( ); // Downcast - runtime error
```

What we need is both a general implementation of a stack
that works for all element types, and a way to easily specialize that stack to a specific element type for increased type
safety and reduced casting and boxing. Generics give us precisely this, by allowing us to parameterize the element type.
Stack<T> has the benefits of both ObjectStack and IntStack.
Like ObjectStack, Stack<T> is written once to work *generally*
across all types. Like IntStack, Stack<T> is *specialized* for a
particular type—the beauty is that this type is T, which we
substitute on the fly.

NOTE

ObjectStack is functionally equivalent to Stack<object>.

Generic Methods

A *generic method* declares generic parameters within the signature of a method.

With generic methods, many fundamental algorithms can be
implemented in only a general-purpose way. Here is a
generic method that swaps two values of any type:

```
static void Swap<T> (ref T a, ref T b)
{
  T temp = a; a = b; b = temp;
}
```

Swap<T> can be used as follows:

```
int x = 5, y = 10;
Swap (ref x, ref y);
```

Generally, there is no need to supply type parameters to a
generic method, because the compiler can implicitly infer the

---

type. If there is ambiguity, generic methods can be called with the type parameters as follows:

```
Swap<int> (ref x, ref y);
```

Within a generic *type*, a method is not classed as generic unless it *introduces* generic parameters (with the angle bracket syntax). The Pop method in our generic stack merely uses the type's existing generic parameter, T, and is not classed as a generic method.

Methods and types are the only constructs that can introduce generic parameters. Properties, indexers, events, fields, methods, operators, and so on cannot declare generic parameters, although they can partake in any generic parameters already declared by their enclosing type. In our generic stack example, for instance, we could write an indexer that returns a generic item:

```
public T this [int index] { get {return data [index];} }
```

Declaring Generic Parameters

Generic parameters can be introduced in the declaration of classes, structs, interfaces, delegates (see the upcoming "Delegates" section), and methods. Other constructs, such as properties, cannot *introduce* a generic parameter, but can *use* a generic parameter. For example, the property Value uses T:

```
public struct Nullable<T>
{
  public T Value {get;}
}
```

A generic type or method can have multiple parameters. For example:

```
class Dictionary<TKeyType, TValueType> {...}
```

To instantiate:

```
Dictionary<int,string> myDic =
  new Dictionary<int,string>();
```

or (in C# 3.0):

```
var myDic = new Dictionary<int,string>();
```

Generic type names and method names can be overloaded as long as the number of generic parameters is different. For example, the following two type names do not conflict:

```
class A<T> {}
class A<T1,T2> {}
```

NOTE

By convention, generic types and methods with a *single* generic parameter typically name their parameter T, as long as the intent of the parameter is clear. When using *multiple* generic parameters, each parameter is prefixed with T, but has a more descriptive name.

---

typeof and Generics

The typeof operator requires specifying the number of parameters when asking for the type of an open type, as follows:

```
class A<T> {}
class A<T1,T2> {}
...

Type a1 = typeof(A<>);
Type a2 = typeof(A<,>);
```

Here is an example of asking for the type of a closed type:

```
Type a3 = typeof(A<int,int>);
```

The default Generic Value

The default keyword can be used to get the default value given a generic type argument. The default value for a reference type is null, and the default value for a value type is the result of bitwise-zeroing the value type's fields:

```
static void Zap<T> (T[] array)
{
  for (int i = 0; i < array.Length; i++)
    array[i] = default(T);
}
```

Generic Constraints

By default, a generic parameter can be substituted with any type whatsoever. *Constraints* can be applied to a generic parameter to require more specific type arguments. These are the possible constraints:

```
where T : base-class      // Base class constraint
where T : interface       // Interface constraint
where T : class           // Class constraint
where T : struct          // Struct constraint
where T : new()           // Parameterless constructor
                          // constraint
where U : T               // Naked type constraint
```

In the following example, GenericClass<T> requires T to derive from SomeClass and implement Interface1:

```
class     SomeClass {}
interface Interface1 {}

class GenericClass<T> where T : SomeClass, Interface1 {}
```

Constraints can be applied wherever generic parameters are defined, in both methods and type definitions.

A *base class constraint* or *interface constraint* specifies that the type parameter must subclass or implement a particular class or interface. This allows instances of that type to be implicitly cast to that class or interface. For example, suppose we want to write a generic Max method that returns the maximum of two values. We can take advantage of the generic interface defined in the System namespace IComparable<T>:

```
public interface IComparable<T>
{
  int CompareTo (T other);
}
```

CompareTo returns a positive number if other is greater than this. Using this interface as a constraint, we can write a Max method as follows (to avoid distraction, null checking is omitted):

```
static T Max <T> (T a, T b) where T : IComparable<T>
{
  return a.CompareTo (b) > 0 ? a : b;
}
```

The Max method can accept arguments of any type implementing IComparable<T> (which includes most built-in types such as int and string):

```
int z = Max (5, 10);              // 10
string last = Max ("ant", "zoo"); // zoo
```

The *class constraint* and *struct constraint* simply specify that T must be a class or a struct. A great example of the struct constraint is the System.Nullable<T> struct (we will discuss this class in depth, later, in the "Nullable Types" section):

```
struct Nullable<T> where T : struct {...}
```

The *parameterless constructor constraint* requires T to have a public parameterless constructor. If this constraint is defined, you can call new( ) on T:

```
static void Initialize<T> (T[] array) where T : new()
{
  for (int i = 0; i < array.Length; i++)
    array[i] = new T( );
}
```

The *naked type constraint* requires one generic parameter to derive from *another generic parameter*. In this example, the method FilteredStack returns another Stack, containing only the subset of elements where the generic parameter T is of the generic parameter U:

```
class Stack<T>
{
  Stack<U> FilteredStack<U>( ) where U : T {...}
}
```

Generics and Covariance

Generic types are not covariant. This means that even if B can be cast to A, T<B> cannot be cast to T<A>. For example, suppose Animal and Bear are defined as follows:

```
class Animal {}
class Bear : Animal {}
```

The following is illegal:

```
Stack<Bear> bears = new Stack <Bear>();

// compile-time error
Stack<Animal> animals = bears;
```

Lack of covariance can hinder reusability. Suppose, for instance, we wanted to write a method to Wash a stack of animals:

```
public class ZooCleaner
{
  public static void Wash (Stack<Animal> animals) {...}
}
```

Calling Wash with a stack of bears would generate a compile-time error. The workaround is to redefine the Wash method with a constraint:

```
public class ZooCleaner
{
  public static void Wash<T> (Stack<T> animals)
    where T : Animal {}
}
```

We can now call Wash as follows:

```
Stack<Bear> bears = new Stack<Bear>();
ZooCleaner.Wash (bears);
```

Subclassing Generic Types

A generic class can be subclassed just like a nongeneric class. The subclass can leave the base class's generic parameters open, as in the following example:

```
class Stack <T>                      {...}
class SpecialStack <T> : Stack <T> {...}
```

Or the subclass can close the generic type parameters with a concrete type:

```
class IntStack : Stack<int> { ... }
```

A subclass can also introduce fresh generic arguments:

```
class Single<T> { ... }
class Double<T,U> : Single<T> { ... }
```

Self-Referencing Generic Declarations

A type can name *itself* as the concrete type when closing a generic argument:

```
public interface IEquatable<T> { bool Equals (T obj); }

public class Balloon : IEquatable<Balloon>
{
  string color;
  int cc;

  public bool Equals (Balloon b)
  {
    if (b == null) return false;
    return b.color == color && b.cc == cc;
  }
}
```

Static Data

Static data is unique for each closed type:

```
class Bob<T> { public static int Count; }

class Test
{
```

```
static void Main( )
{
  Console.WriteLine (++Bob<int>.Count);      // 1
  Console.WriteLine (++Bob<int>.Count);      // 2
  Console.WriteLine (++Bob<string>.Count);   // 1
  Console.WriteLine (++Bob<object>.Count);   // 1
}
}
```

Generic Collection Initialization

You can instantiate and populate a generic collection in a single step, as follows:

```
using System.Collections.Generic;
...

List<int> list = new List<int> {1, 2, 3};
```

The compiler translates this to:

```
using System.Collections.Generic;
...

List<int> list = new List<int>( );
list.Add (1); list.Add (2); list.Add (3);
```

This requires that the collection implements the ICollection<T> interface, defined in System.Collections. Generic—the standard .NET interface for mutable collections.

Delegates

A delegate dynamically wires up a method caller to its target method. There are two aspects to a delegate: *type* and *instance*. A *delegate type* defines a *protocol* to which the caller and target will conform, comprising a list of parameter types and a return type. A *delegate instance* refers to one or more target methods conforming to that protocol.

A delegate instance literally acts as a delegate for the caller: the caller invokes the delegate, and then the delegate calls the target method. This indirection decouples the caller from the target method.

A delegate type declaration is preceded by the keyword delegate, but otherwise it resembles an (abstract) method declaration. For example:

```
delegate int Transformer (int x);
```

To create a delegate instance, you can assign a method to a delegate variable:

```
class Test
{
  static void Main()
  {
    Transformer t = Square;  // Create delegate instance
    int result = t(3);       // Invoke delegate
    Console.Write (result);  // 9
  }
  static int Square (int x) { return x * x; }
}
```

Invoking a delegate is just like invoking a method (as the delegate's purpose is merely to provide a level of indirection):

```
t(3);
```

The statement:

```
Transformer t = Square;
```

is shorthand for:

```
Transformer t = new Transformer(Square);
```

NOTE

A delegate is similar to a "callback," a general term that captures constructs such as C function pointers.

Writing Plug-in Methods with Delegates

A delegate variable is assigned a method *dynamically*. This is useful for writing plug-in methods. In this example, we have a utility method named Transform, which applies a transform to each element in an integer array. The Transform method has a delegate parameter for specifying a plug-in transform.

```
public delegate int Transformer (int x);

public class Util
{
  public static void Transform (int[] values,
                                Transformer t)
  {
    for (int i = 0; i < values.Length; i++)
      values[i] = t(values[i]);
  }
}

class Test
{
  static void Main( )
  {
    int[] values = new int[] {1, 2, 3};
    Util.Transform(values, Square);    // Dynamically
                                       // hook in Square
    foreach (int i in values)
      Console.Write (i + "  ");        // 1  4  9
  }

  static int Square (int x) { return x * x; }
}
```

Multicast Delegates

All delegate instances have *multicast* capability. This means that a delegate instance can reference not just a single target method, but also a list of target methods. The += operator combines delegate instances. For example:

```
SomeDelegate d = SomeMethod1;
d += SomeMethod2;
```

Invoking d will now call both SomeMethod1 and SomeMethod2. Delegates are invoked in the order they are added.

The -= method removes the right delegate operand from the left delegate operand. For example:

```
d -= SomeMethod1;
```

Invoking d will now cause only SomeMethod2 to be invoked.

Calling += on a delegate variable with a null value works, and it is equivalent to assigning the variable to a new value:

```
SomeDelegate d = null;
d += SomeMethod1;        // Equivalent (when d is
                         // null) to d = SomeMethod1;
```

NOTE

All delegate types implicitly inherit System.MulticastDelegate, which inherits from System.Delegate. C# compiles += and -= operations made on a delegate to the static Combine and Remove methods of the System.Delegate class.

If a multicast delegate has a nonvoid return type, the caller receives the return value from the last method to be invoked. The preceding methods are still called, but their return values are discarded. In most scenarios in which multicast delegates are used, they have void return types, so this subtlety does not arise.

Instance Versus Static Method Targets

When a delegate instance is assigned to an instance method, the delegate instance maintains a reference not only to the method, but also to the *instance* of that method. (The System.Delegate class's Target property represents this instance and will be null for a delegate referencing a static method.)

Generic Delegate Types

A delegate type may contain generic type parameters. For example:

```
public delegate T Transformer<T> (T arg);
```

Here's how we could use this delegate type:

```
static double Square (double x) { return x * x; }

static void Main()
{
  Transformer<double> s = Square;
  Console.WriteLine (s (3.3));          // 10.89
}
```

Delegate Compatibility

Type compatibility

Delegate types are all incompatible with each other, even if their signatures are the same:

```
delegate void D1();
delegate void D2();
...

D1 d1 = Method1;
D2 d2 = d1;                            // compile-time error
```

Delegate instances are considered equal if they have the same method targets:

```
delegate void D();
...

D d1 = Method1;
D d2 = Method1;
Console.WriteLine (d1 == d2);          // true
```

Parameter compatibility

When you call a method, you can supply arguments that have more specific types than the parameters of that method. This is ordinary polymorphic behavior. For exactly the same reason, a delegate can have more specific parameter types than its method target. This is called *contravariance*.

Here's an example:

```
delegate void SpecificDelegate (SpecificClass s);

class SpecificClass { }
```

```
static void Main()
{
  SpecificDelegate specificDelegate = GeneralHandler;
  specificDelegate (new SpecificClass());
}

static void GeneralHandler (object o)
{
  Console.WriteLine (o.GetType());  // SpecificClass
}
```

NOTE

The standard event pattern is designed to help you lever-
age contravariance through its use of the common
EventArgs base class. For example, you can have a single
method invoked by two different delegates, one passing a
MouseEventArgs and the other passing a KeyEventArgs.

Return type compatibility

If you call a method, you may get back a type that is more
specific than what you asked for. This is ordinary polymorphic behavior. For exactly the same reason, the return type of
a delegate can be less specific than the return type of its target method. This is called *covariance*. For example:

```
delegate Asset DebtCollector();

class Asset { }
class House : Asset { }

static void Main()
{
    DebtCollector d = new DebtCollector (GetHomeSweetHome);
    Asset a = d();
    Console.WriteLine (a.GetType());    // House
}
static House GetHomeSweetHome() { return new House(); }
```

The DebtCollector expects to get back an Asset—but any
Asset will do: delegate return types are *covariant*.

Events

When using delegates, two emergent roles commonly appear: broadcaster and subscriber.

The *broadcaster* is a type that contains a delegate field. It decides when to broadcast by invoking the delegate.

The *subscribers* are the method target recipients. A subscriber decides when to start and stop listening by calling += and -= on the broadcaster's delegate. A subscriber does not know about, or interfere with, other subscribers.

Events are a language feature that formalizes this pattern. An event is a wrapper for a delegate that exposes just the subset of delegate features required for the broadcaster/subscriber model. The main purpose of events is to *prevent subscribers from interfering with one another*.

To declare an event member, you put the event keyword in front of a delegate member. For instance:

```
public class Broadcaster
{
  public event ProgressReporter Progress;
}
```

Code within the Broadcaster type has full access to Progress and can treat it as a delegate. Code outside of Broadcaster can only perform += and -= operations on Progress.

Consider the following example. The Stock class invokes its PriceChanged event every time the Price of the Stock changes:

```
public delegate void PriceChangedHandler
  (decimal oldPrice, decimal newPrice);

public class Stock
{
  string symbol;
  decimal price;

  public Stock (string symbol) {this.symbol = symbol;}
```

```
    public event PriceChangedHandler PriceChanged;

    public decimal Price
    {
      get { return price; }
      set
      {
        if (price == value) return;
        if (PriceChanged != null)
          PriceChanged (price, value);    // Fire event
        price = value;
      }
    }
  }
```

If we removed the event keyword from our example so that PriceChanged became an ordinary delegate field, our example would give the same results. However, Stock would be less robust, in that subscribers could do the following things to interfere with one another:

- Replace other subscribers by reassigning PriceChanged (instead of using the += operator).
- Clear all subscribers by setting PriceChanged to null.
- Broadcast to other subscribers by invoking the delegate.

Standard Event Pattern

The .NET Framework defines a standard pattern for writing events. Its purpose is to provide consistency across both Framework and user code. Here's the preceding example refactored with this pattern:

```
using System;

public class PriceChangedEventArgs : EventArgs
{
  public readonly decimal LastPrice;
  public readonly decimal NewPrice;

  public PriceChangedEventArgs (decimal lastPrice,
                                decimal newPrice)
  {
    LastPrice = lastPrice; NewPrice = newPrice;
```

```
    }
  }

  public class Stock
  {
    string symbol;
    decimal price;

    public Stock (string symbol) {this.symbol = symbol;}

    public event EventHandler<PriceChangedEventArgs>
                  PriceChanged;

    protected virtual void OnPriceChanged
                            (PriceChangedEventArgs e)
    {
      if (PriceChanged != null) PriceChanged (this, e);
    }

    public decimal Price
    {
      get { return price; }
      set
      {
        if (price == value) return;
        OnPriceChanged (new PriceChangedEventArgs (price,
                                                   value));
        price = value;
      }
    }
  }
```

At the core of the standard event pattern is System.EventArgs:
a predefined Framework class with no members (other than
the static Empty property). EventArgs is a base class for con-
veying information for an event. In this example, we subclass EventArgs to convey the old and new prices when a
PriceChanged event is fired.

The generic System.EventHandler delegate is also part of the
.NET Framework and is defined as follows:

```
    public delegate void EventHandler<TEventArgs>
      (object source, TEventArgs e)
      where TEventArgs : EventArgs;
```

A protected virtual method, named On-*event-name*, centralizes firing of the event. This allows subclasses to fire the event (which is usually desirable) and allows subclasses to insert code before and after the event is fired.

Here's how we could use our Stock class:

```
static void Main()
{
  Stock stock = new Stock ("THPW");
  stock.Price = 27.10M;

  stock.PriceChanged += stock_PriceChanged;
  stock.Price = 31.59M;
}

static void stock_PriceChanged
  (object sender, PriceChangedEventArgs e)
{
  if ((e.NewPrice - e.LastPrice) / e.LastPrice > 0.1M)
    Console.WriteLine ("Alert, 10% price increase!");
}
```

For events that don't carry additional information, the Framework also provides a nongeneric EventHandler delegate. We can demonstrate this by rewriting our Stock class such that the PriceChanged event fires *after* the price changes. This means that no additional information need be transmitted with the event:

```
public class Stock
{
  string symbol;
  decimal price;

  public Stock (string symbol) {this.symbol = symbol;}

  public event EventHandler PriceChanged;

  protected virtual void OnPriceChanged (EventArgs e)
  {
    if (PriceChanged != null) PriceChanged (this, e);
  }

  public decimal Price
  {
    get { return price; }
    set
    {
      if (price == value) return;
      price = value;
      OnPriceChanged (EventArgs.Empty);
    }
  }
}
```

Note that we also used the EventArgs.Empty property—this saves instantiating an instance of EventArgs.

Event Accessors

An event's *accessors* are the implementations of its += and -= functions. By default, accessors are implemented implicitly by the compiler. Consider this event declaration:

```
public event EventHandler PriceChanged;
```

The compiler converts this to:

- A private delegate field
- A public pair of event accessor functions, whose implementations forward the += and -= operations to the private delegate field

You can take over this process by defining *explicit* event accessors. Here is a manual implementation of the PriceChanged event from our previous example:

```
private EventHandler _PriceChanged;  // private delegate

public event EventHandler PriceChanged
{
  add    { _PriceChanged += value;  }
  remove { _PriceChanged -= value;  }
}
```

This example is functionally identical to C#'s default accessor implementation. The add and remove keywords after the event declaration instruct C# not to generate a default field and accessor logic.

With explicit event accessors, you can apply more complex strategies to the storage and access of the underlying delegate. There are three scenarios where this is useful:

- When the event accessors are merely relays for another class that is broadcasting the event.

- When the class exposes a large number of events, where most of the time very few subscribers exist, such as a Windows control. In such cases, it is better to store the subscriber's delegate instances in a dictionary, as a dictionary will contain less storage overhead than dozens of null delegate field references.

- When explicitly implementing an interface that declares an event.

Here is an example that illustrates the last point:

```
public interface IFoo { event EventHandler Ev; }

class Foo : IFoo
{
  private EventHandler ev;
  event EventHandler IFoo.Ev
  {
    add { ev += value; } remove { ev -= value; }
  }
}
```

Event Modifiers

Like methods, events can be virtual, overridden, abstract, and sealed. Events can also be static.

Lambda Expressions (C# 3.0)

A *lambda expression* is an unnamed method written in place of a delegate instance. The compiler immediately converts the lambda expression to either:

- A delegate instance.
- An *expression tree*, of type Expression<TDelegate>, representing the code inside the lambda expression in a traversable object model. This allows the lambda expression to be interpreted later at runtime (we describe the process in Chapter 8 of *C# 3.0 in a Nutshell*).

Given the following delegate type:

```
delegate int Transformer (int i);
```

we could assign and invoke the lambda expression x => x * x as follows:

```
Transformer sqr = x => x * x;
Console.WriteLine (sqr(3));    // 9
```

NOTE

Internally, the compiler resolves lambda expressions of this type by writing a private method and moving the expression's code into that method.

A lambda expression has the following form:

```
(parameters) => expression-or-statement-block
```

For convenience, you can omit the parentheses if and only if there is exactly one parameter of an inferable type.

In our example, there is a single parameter, x, and the expression is x * x:

```
x => x * x;
```

Each parameter of the lambda expression corresponds to a delegate parameter, and the type of the expression (which may be void) corresponds to the return type of the delegate.

In our example, x corresponds to parameter i, and the expression x * x corresponds to the return type int, therefore being compatible with the Transformer delegate:

```
delegate int Transformer (int i);
```

A lambda expression's code can be a *statement block* instead of an expression. We can rewrite our example as follows:

```
x => {return x * x;};
```

Explicitly Specifying Lambda Parameter Types

The compiler can usually *infer* the type of lambda parameters contextually. When this is not the case, you must explicitly specify the type of each parameter. Consider the following delegate type:

```
delegate int Transformer (int i);
```

The compiler uses type inference to infer that x is an int by examining Transfomer's parameter type:

```
Transformer d = x => x * x;
```

We could explicitly specify x's type as follows:

```
Transformer d = (int x) => x * x;
```

Generic Lambda Expressions and the Func Delegates

With generic delegates, it becomes possible to write a small set of delegate types that are so general they can work for methods of any return type and any (reasonable) number of arguments.

These delegates are the Func and Action delegates, defined in the System namespace.

Here are the Func delegates (notice that TResult is always the last type parameter):

```
delegate TResult Func <T> ();

delegate TResult Func <T, TResult>
                (T arg1);

delegate TResult Func <T1, T2, TResult>
                (T1 arg1, T2 arg2);

delegate TResult Func <T1, T2, T3, TResult>
                (T1 arg1, T2 arg2, T3 arg3);

delegate TResult Func <T1, T2, T3, T4, TResult>
                (T1 arg1, T2 arg2, T3 arg3, T4 arg4);
```

Here are the Action delegates:

```
delegate void Action();

delegate void Action <T>
                (T arg1);

delegate void Action <T1, T2>
                (T1 arg1, T2 arg2);

delegate void Action <T1, T2, T3>
                (T1 arg1, T2 arg2, T3 arg3);

delegate void Action <T1, T2, T3, T4>
                (T1 arg1, T2 arg2, T3 arg3,
                                   T4 arg4);
```

These delegates are extremely general. The Transformer dele-gate in our previous example can be replaced with a Func delegate that takes a single int argument and returns an int value:

```
Func<int,int> sqr = x => x * x;
Console.WriteLine (sqr(3));      // 9
```

Outer Variables

A lambda expression can reference the local variables and parameters of the method in which it's defined. For example:

```
static void Main()
{
  int factor = 2;
  Func<int, int> multiplier = n => n * factor;
  Console.WriteLine (multiplier (3));        // 6
}
```

Local variables and parameters referenced by a lambda expression are called *outer variables* or *captured variables*. A lambda expression that includes outer variables is called a *closure*.

Outer variables are evaluated when the delegate is actually *invoked*, not when the variables are *captured*:

```
int factor = 2;
Func<int, int> multiplier = n => n * factor;
factor = 10;
Console.WriteLine (multiplier (2));        // 20
```

Lambda expressions can update captured variables:

```
int seed = 0;
Func<int> natural = () => seed++;
Console.WriteLine (natural());        // 0
Console.WriteLine (natural());        // 1
```

Outer variables have their lifetimes extended to that of the delegate. In the following example, the local variable seed would ordinarily disappear from scope when Natural finished executing. But because seed has been captured, its lifetime is extended to that of the capturing delegate, natural:

```
static Func<int> Natural()
{
  int seed = 0;
  return () => seed++;     // Returns a closure
}

static void Main()
{
  Func<int> natural = Natural();
```

```
    Console.WriteLine (natural());       // 0
    Console.WriteLine (natural());       // 1
  }
```

A local variable *instantiated* within a lambda expression is unique per invocation of the delegate instance. If we refactor our previous example to instantiate seed *within* the lambda expression, we get a different (in this case, undesirable) result:

```
static Func<int> Natural()
{
  return() => { int seed = 0; return seed++; };
}

static void Main()
{
  NumericSequence natural = Natural();
  Console.WriteLine (natural());        // 0
  Console.WriteLine (natural());        // 0
}
```

Anonymous Methods

Anonymous methods are a C# 2.0 feature that has been sub-sumed by C# 3.0 lambda expressions. An anonymous method is like a lambda expression, but it lacks the following features:

- Implicitly typed parameters
- Expression syntax (an anonymous method must always be a statement block)
- The ability to compile to an expression tree by assigning to Expression<T>

To write an anonymous method, include the delegate key-word, followed by a parameter declaration and then a method body. For example, given this delegate:

```
delegate int Transformer (int i);
```

we could write and call an anonymous method as follows:

```
Transformer sqr = delegate (int x) {return x * x;};
Console.WriteLine (sqr(3));    // 9
```

The first line is semantically equivalent to the following
lambda expression:

```
Transformer sqr =            (int x) => {return x * x;};
```

Or simply:

```
Transformer sqr =            x  => x * x;
```

Anonymous methods capture outer variables in the same
way lambda expressions do.

try Statements and Exceptions

A try statement specifies a code block subject to error-
handling or clean-up code. The try *block* must be followed
by a catch *block*, a finally *block*, or both. The catch block
executes when an error occurs in the try block. The finally
block executes after execution leaves the try block (or if
present, the catch block), to perform clean-up code, whether
or not an error occurred.

A catch block has access to an Exception object, which contains information about the error. You use a catch block to
either compensate for the error or *rethrow* the exception. You
rethrow an exception if you merely want to log the problem,
or if you want to rethrow a new, higher-level exception type.

A finally block adds determinism to your program by
always executing no matter what. It's useful for clean-up
tasks such as closing network connections.

A try statement looks like this:

```
try
{
  ... // exception may get thrown within execution of
      // this block
}
catch (ExceptionA ex)
{
  ... // handle exception of type ExceptionA
}
```

```
catch (ExceptionB ex)
{
  ... // handle exception of type ExceptionB
}
finally
{
  ... // clean-up code
}
```

Consider the following program:

```
static void Main()
{
  int x = 3, y = 0;
  Console.WriteLine (x / y);
}
```

y is zero, so the runtime throws a DivideByZeroException, and our program terminates. We can prevent this by catching the exception as follows:

```
static void Main()
{
  try
  {
    int x = 3, y = 0;
    Console.WriteLine (x / y);
  }
  catch (DivideByZeroException ex)
  {
    Console.WriteLine ("y cannot be zero");
  }
  Console.WriteLine ("program completed");
}

OUTPUT:
x cannot be zero
program completed
```

When an exception is thrown, the CLR performs a test:

Is execution currently within a try *statement that can catch the exception?*

- If so, execution is passed to the compatible catch block. If the catch block successfully finishes executing, execution moves to the next statement after the `try` statement (if present, executing the `finally` block first).

- If not, execution jumps back to the caller of the function, and the test is repeated (after executing any `finally` blocks that wrap the statement).

If no function takes responsibility for the exception, an error dialog is displayed to the user, and the program terminates.

The catch Clause

A catch clause specifies what type of exception to catch. This must either be `System.Exception` or a subclass of `System.Exception`.

Catching `System.Exception` catches all possible errors. This is useful when:

- Your program can potentially recover, regardless of the specific exception type.
- You plan to rethrow the exception (perhaps after logging it).
- Your error handler is the last resort, prior to termination of the program.

More typically, though, you catch *specific exception types* to avoid having to deal with circumstances for which your handler wasn't designed (e.g., an `OutOfMemoryException`).

You can handle multiple exception types with multiple catch clauses:

```
try
{
  DoSomething();
}
catch (IndexOutOfRangeException ex) { ... }
catch (FormatException ex)          { ... }
catch (OverflowException ex)        { ... }
```

Only one catch clause executes for a given exception. If you want to include a safety net to catch more general exceptions (such as System.Exception), you must put the more specific handlers *first*.

An exception can be caught without specifying a variable, if you don't need to access its properties:

```
catch (StackOverflowException)   // no variable
  { ... }
```

Furthermore, you can omit both the variable and the type (meaning that all exceptions will be caught):

```
catch { ... }
```

The finally Block

A finally block always executes—whether or not an exception is thrown, and whether or not the try block runs to completion. finally blocks are typically used for cleanup code.

A finally block executes:

- After a catch block finishes
- After control leaves the try block because of a jump statement (e.g., return or goto)
- After the try block ends

A finally block helps add determinism to a program. In the following example, the file that we open *always* gets closed, regardless of whether:

- The try block finishes normally.
- Execution returns early, as the file is empty (EndOfStream).
- An IOException is thrown while reading the file.

```
static void ReadFile()
{
  StreamReader reader = null;  // In System.IO
  try
  {
    reader = File.OpenText ("file.txt");
    if (reader.EndOfStream) return;
```

```
            Console.WriteLine (reader.ReadToEnd());
      }
      finally
      {
        if (reader != null) reader.Dispose();
      }
    }
```

In this example, we closed the file by calling Dispose on the StreamReader. Calling Dispose on an object, within a finally block, is a standard convention throughout the .NET Framework and is supported explicitly in C# through the using statement.

The using statement

Many classes encapsulate unmanaged resources, such as file handles, graphics handles, or database connections. These classes implement System.IDisposable, which defines a single parameterless method named Dispose to clean up these resources. The using statement provides an elegant syntax for calling Dispose on an IDisposable object within a finally block.

The following:

```
    using (StreamReader reader = File.OpenText (
          "file.txt"))
    {
      ...
    }
```

is precisely equivalent to:

```
    StreamReader reader = File.OpenText ("file.txt");
    try
    {
      ...
    }
    finally
    {
      if (reader != null)
        ((IDisposable)reader).Dispose();
    }
```

Throwing Exceptions

Exceptions can be thrown either by the runtime, or in user code. In this example, Display throws a System. ArgumentNullException:

```
static void Display (string name)
{
  if (name == null)
    throw new ArgumentNullException ("name");

  Console.WriteLine (name);
}

static void Main()
{
  try { Display (null); }
  catch (ArgumentNullException ex)
  {
    Console.WriteLine ("Caught the exception");
  }
}
```

Rethrowing an exception

You can capture and rethrow an exception as follows:

```
try {  ...  }
catch (Exception ex)
{
  // Log error
  ...
  throw;          // Rethrow same exception
}
```

Rethrowing in this manner lets you log an error without *swallowing* it. It also lets you back out of handling an exception should circumstances be outside what you expected.

The other common scenario is to rethrow a more specific exception type. For example:

```
try
{
  ... // parse a date of birth from XML element data
}
```

```
catch (FormatException ex)
{
    throw new XmlException ("Invalid date of birth", ex);
}
```

Rethrowing an exception does not affect the StackTrace property of the exception (see the next section). When rethrowing a different exception, you can set the InnerException property with the original exception if doing so could aid debugging. Nearly all types of exceptions provide a constructor for this.

Key Properties of System.Exception

The following are the most important properties of System. Exception:

StackTrace
> A string representing all the methods that are called from the origin of the exception to the catch block.

Message
> A string with a description of the error.

InnerException
> The inner exception (if any) that caused the outer exception. This, itself, may have another InnerException.

NOTE

All exceptions in C# are runtime exceptions—there is no equivalent to Java's compile-time checked exceptions.

Common Exception Types

The following exception types are used widely throughout the CLR and .NET Framework. You can throw these yourself, or use them as base classes for deriving custom exception types.

`System.ArgumentException`

Thrown when a function is called with a bogus argument. This generally indicates a program bug.

`System.ArgumentNullException`

Thrown when a function argument is (unexpectedly) null. (It is a subclass of `ArgumentException`.

`System.ArgumentOutOfRangeException`

Thrown when a (usually numeric) argument is too big or too small. (It is also a subclass of `ArgumentException`.) For example, this is thrown when passing a negative number into a function that accepts only positive values.

`System.InvalidOperationException`

Thrown when the state of an object is unsuitable for a method to successfully execute, regardless of any particular argument values. Examples include reading an unopened file or getting the next element from an enumerator where the underlying list has been modified partway through the iteration.

`System.NotSupportedException`

Thrown to indicate that a particular functionality is not supported. A good example is calling the `Add` method on a collection for which `IsReadOnly` returns `true`.

`System.NotImplementedException`

Thrown to indicate that a function has not yet been implemented.

`System.ObjectDisposedException`

Thrown when the object upon which the function is called has been disposed.

Enumeration and Iterators

Enumeration

An *enumerator* is a read-only, forward-only cursor over a *sequence of values*. An enumerator is an object that either:

- Implements IEnumerator or IEnumerator<T>
- Has a method named MoveNext for iterating the sequence, and a property called Current for getting the current element in the sequence

The foreach statement iterates over an *enumerable* object. An enumerable object is the logical representation of a sequence, and is not itself a cursor, but an object that produces cursors over itself. An enumerable object either:

- Implements IEnumerable or IEnumerable<T>
- Has a method named GetEnumerator that returns an enumerator

---

NOTE

IEnumerator and IEnumerable are defined in System. Collections. IEnumerator<T> and IEnumerable<T> are defined in System.Collections.Generic.

The enumeration pattern is as follows:

```
class Enumerator      // typically implements IEnumerator
                      // or IEnumerator<T>
{
  public IteratorVariableType Current { get {...} }
  public bool MoveNext()             {...}
}

class Enumerable      // typically implements IEnumerable
                      // or IEnumerable<T>
{
  public Enumerator GetEnumerator() {...}
}
```

Here is the high-level way of iterating through the characters in the word "beer" using a foreach statement:

```
foreach (char c in "beer")
  Console.WriteLine (c);
```

Here is the low-level way of iterating through the characters in the word "beer" without using a foreach statement:

```
var enumerator = "beer".GetEnumerator();

while (enumerator.MoveNext())
{
  var element = enumerator.Current;
  Console.WriteLine (element);
}
```

The foreach statement also acts as a using statement, implicitly disposing the enumerator object.

Iterators

Whereas a foreach statement is a *consumer* of an enumerator, an iterator is a *producer* of an enumerator. In this example, we use an iterator to return a sequence of Fibonacci numbers (where each number is the sum of the previous two):

```
using System;
using System.Collections.Generic;

class Test
{
  static void Main()
  {
    foreach (int fib in Fibs(6))
      Console.Write (fib + " ");
  }

  static IEnumerable<int> Fibs(int fibCount)
  {
    for (int i = 0, prevFib = 1, curFib = 1;
         i < fibCount;
         i++)
```

```
      {
        yield return prevFib;
        int newFib = prevFib+curFib;
        prevFib = curFib;
        curFib = newFib;
      }
   }
}
```

   OUTPUT: 1 1 2 3 5 8

Whereas a return statement expresses "Here's the value you asked me to return from this method," a yield return statement expresses "Here's the next element you asked me to yield from this enumerator." On each yield statement, control is returned to the caller, but the callee's state is maintained so that the method can continue executing as soon as the caller enumerates the next element. The lifetime of this state is bound to the enumerator, such that the state can be released when the caller has finished enumerating.

WARNING

The compiler converts iterator methods into private classes that implement IEnumerable<T> and IEnumerator<T>. The logic within the iterator block is "inverted" and spliced into the MoveNext method and Current property on the compiler-written enumerator class. This means that when you call an iterator method, all you're doing is instantiating the compiler-written class; none of your code actually runs! Your code runs only when you start enumerating over the resultant sequence, typically with a foreach statement.

Iterator Semantics

An iterator is a method, property, or indexer that contains one or more yield statements. An iterator must return one of the following four interfaces (otherwise, the compiler will generate an error):

```
// Enumerable interfaces
System.Collections.IEnumerable
System.Collections.Generic.IEnumerable<T>

// Enumerator interfaces
System.Collections.IEnumerator
System.Collections.Generic.IEnumerator<T>
```

Iterators that return an *enumerator* interface tend to be used less often. They're useful when writing a custom collection class: typically, you name the iterator GetEnumerator and have your class implement IEnumerable<T>.

Iterators that return an *enumerable* interface are more common—and simpler to use because you don't have to write a collection class. The compiler, behind the scenes, writes a private class implementing IEnumerable<T> (as well as IEnumerator<T>).

Multiple yield statements

In iterator can include multiple yield statements. For example:

```
static void Main()
{
  foreach (string s in Foo())
    Console.Write (s + " ");   // One Two Three
}

static IEnumerable<string> Foo()
{
  yield return "One";
  yield return "Two";
  yield return "Three";
}
```

yield break

The yield break statement indicates that the iterator block should exit early, without returning more elements. We can modify the preceding Foo method to demonstrate:

```
static IEnumerable<string> Foo(bool breakEarly)
{
  yield return "One";
  yield return "Two";

  if (breakEarly)
    yield break;

  yield return "Three";
}
```

WARNING

A return statement is illegal in an iterator block—you must use yield break instead.

Composing Sequences

Iterators are highly composable. We can extend our example, this time to output only even Fibonacci numbers:

```
using System;
using System.Collections.Generic;

class Test
{
  static void Main()
  {
    foreach (int fib in EvenNumbersOnly (Fibs (6)))
      Console.WriteLine(fib);
  }

  static IEnumerable<int> Fibs (int fibCount)
  {
    for (int i = 0, prevFib = 1, curFib = 1;
         i < fibCount;
         i++)
    {
      yield return prevFib;
      int newFib = prevFib+curFib;
      prevFib = curFib;
      curFib = newFib;
    }
  }
```

```
static IEnumerable<int> EvenNumbersOnly (
                        IEnumerable<int> sequence)
{
  foreach(int x in sequence)
    if ((x % 2) == 0)
      yield return x;
}
```

Each element is not calculated until the last moment—when
requested by a MoveNext() operation. Figure 5 shows the
data requests and data output over time.

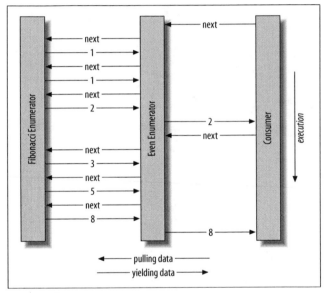

Figure 5. Composing sequences

The composability of the iterator pattern is extremely useful
in building LINQ queries.

Nullable Types

Null Basics

Reference types can represent a nonexistent value with a null reference. Value types, however, cannot ordinarily represent null values. For example:

```
string s = null;      // OK, Reference Type
int i = null;         // Compile Error, Value Type
                      // cannot be null
```

To represent null in a value type, you must use a special construct called a *nullable type*. A nullable type is denoted with a value type followed by the ? symbol:

```
int? i = null;                    // OK, Nullable Type
Console.WriteLine (i == null);    // True
```

Nullable<T> struct

T? translates into System.Nullable<T>. Nullable<T> is a lightweight immutable struct, having only two fields to represent Value and HasValue. The essence of System.Nullable<T> is very simple:

```
public struct Nullable<T> where T : struct
{
  public T Value {get;}
  public bool HasValue {get;}
  public T GetValueOrDefault();
  public T GetValueOrDefault(T defaultValue);
  ...
}
```

The code:

```
int? i = null;
Console.WriteLine (i == null);            // true
```

gets translated by the compiler to:

```
Nullable<int> i = new Nullable<int>();
Console.WriteLine (! i.HasValue);         // true
```

Attempting to retrieve Value when HasValue is false throws an InvalidOperationException. GetValueOrDefault() returns Value if HasValue is true; otherwise, it returns new T() or a specified a custom default value.

The default value of T? is null.

Implicit and explicit nullable conversions

The conversion from T to T? is implicit, and from T? to T is explicit. For example:

```
int? x = 5;        // implicit
int y = (int)x;    // explicit
```

The explicit cast is directly equivalent to calling the nullable object's Value property. Hence, if HasValue is false, an InvalidOperationException is thrown.

Boxing and unboxing nullable values

When T? is boxed, the boxed value on the heap contains T, not T?. This optimization is possible because a boxed value is a reference type that can already express null.

Lifted Operators

The Nullable<T> struct does not define operators such as <, >, or even ==. Despite this, the following code compiles and executes correctly:

```
int? x = 5;
int? y = 10;
bool b = x < y;    // true
```

This works because the compiler steals or "lifts" the less-than operator from the underlying value type. Semantically, it translates the preceding comparison expression into this:

```
bool b = (x.HasValue && y.HasValue)
         ? (x.Value < y.Value)
         : false;
```

In other words, if both x and y have values, it compares via int's less-than operator; otherwise, it returns false.

Operator lifting means you can implicitly use T's operators on T?. You can define operators for T? to provide special-purpose null behavior, but in the vast majority of cases, it's best to rely on the compiler automatically applying systematic nullable logic for you. The compiler performs null logic differently depending on the category of operator.

Equality operators (== !=)

Lifted equality operators handle nulls just like reference types do. This means two null values are equal:

```
Console.Write (          null ==          null);   // True
Console.Write ((bool?)null == (bool?)null);   // True
```

Further:

- If exactly one operand is null, the operands are unequal.
- If both operands are nonnull, their Values are compared.

Relational operators (< <= >= >)

The relational operators work on the principle that it is meaningless to compare null operands. This means comparing a null value to either a null or nonnull value returns false.

```
bool b = x < y;   // Translation:

bool b = (x == null || y == null)
         ? false
         : (x.Value < y.Value);
```

All other operators (+ - * / % & | ^ << >> + ++ - -- ! ~)

These operators return null when any operands are null. (This pattern should be familiar to SQL users.)

```
int? c = x + y;   // Translation:
```

```
int? c = (x == null || y == null)
         ? null
         : (int?) (x.Value + y.Value);
```

Mixing nullable and nonnullable operators

You can mix and match nullable and nonnullable types (this
works because there is an implicit conversion from T to T?):

```
int? x = null;
int y = 2;
int? z = x + y;    // equivalent to x + (int?)y
```

bool?

When supplied operands of type bool?, the & and | operators
treat null as an *unknown value*. So, null | true is true because:

- If the unknown value was false, the result would be true.
- If the unknown value was true, the result would be true.

Similarly, null & false is false. This behavior would be familiar to SQL users. The following example enumerates other
combinations:

```
bool? n = null;
bool? f = false;
bool? t = true;
Console.WriteLine (n | n);    // (null)
Console.WriteLine (n | f);    // (null)
Console.WriteLine (n | t);    // True
Console.WriteLine (n & n);    // (null)
Console.WriteLine (n & f);    // False
Console.WriteLine (n & t);    // (null)
```

Null Coalescing Operator

The ?? operator is the null coalescing operator, and it can be
used with both nullable types and reference types. It says, "If
the operand is nonnull, give it to me; otherwise, give me a
default value." For example:

```
int? x = null;
int y = x ?? 5;        // y is 5
```

The ?? operator is equivalent to calling GetValueOrDefault with an explicit default value.

Operator Overloading

Operators can be overloaded to provide more natural syntax for custom types. Operator overloading is most appropriately used for implementing custom structs that represent fairly primitive data types. For example, a custom numeric type is an excellent candidate for operator overloading.

The overloadable symbolic operators are as follows:

+ (unary)	- (unary)	!	~	++
--	+	-	*	/
%	&	|	^	<<
>>	==	!=	>	<
>=	<=			

The following operators are also overloadable:

- Implicit and explicit conversions (with the implicit and explicit keywords)
- The literals true and false

The following operators are indirectly overloaded:

- The compound assignment operators (e.g., +=, /=) are implicitly overridden by overriding the noncompound operators (e.g., +, =).
- The conditional operators && and || are implicitly overridden by overriding the bitwise operators & and |.

Operator Functions

An operator is overloaded by declaring an *operator function*. An operator function has the following rules:

- The name of the function is specified with the operator keyword followed by an operator symbol.
- The operator function must be marked static.
- The parameters of the operator function represent the operands.
- The return type of an operator function represents the result of an expression.
- At least one of the operands must be the type in which the operator function is declared.

In the following example, we define a struct called Note representing a musical note, and then overload the + operator:

```
public struct Note
{
  int value;

  public Note (int semitonesFromA)
   { value = semitonesFromA; }

  public static Note operator + (Note x, int semitones)
  {
    return new Note (x.value + semitones);
  }
}
```

This overload allows us to add an int to a Note:

```
Note B = new Note(2);
Note CSharp = B + 2;
```

Overloading an assignment operator automatically supports the corresponding compound assignment operator. In our example, because we overrode +, we can use += too:

```
CSharp += 2;
```

Overloading Equality and Comparison Operators

Equality and comparison operators are sometimes overridden when writing structs, and in rare cases when writing classes. Special rules and obligations come with overloading the equality and comparison operators:

Pairing

> The C# compiler enforces that operators that are logical pairs are both defined. These operators are (== !=), (< >), and (<= >=).

Equals *and* GetHashCode

> If you overload == and !=, you will usually need to override object's Equals and GetHashCode methods so that collections and hashtables will work reliably with the type.

IComparable *and* IComparable<T>

> If you overload (< >) and (<= >=), you would also typically implement IComparable and IComparable<T>.

Extending the previous example, here's how we could overload Note's equality operators:

```
public static bool operator == (Note n1, Note n2)
{
    return n1.value == n2.value;
}
public static bool operator != (Note n1, Note n2)
{
    return !(n1.value == n2.value);
}
public override bool Equals (object otherNote)
{
    if (!(otherNote is Note)) return false;
    return this == (Note)otherNote;
}
public override int GetHashCode()
{
    return value.GetHashCode();   // Use value's hashcode
}
```

Custom Implicit and Explicit Conversions

Implicit and explicit conversions are overloadable operators. These conversions are typically overloaded to make converting between strongly related types (such as numeric types) concise and natural.

To convert between weakly related types, the following strategies are more suitable:

- Write a constructor that has a parameter of the type to convert from.
- Write To*XXX* and From*XXX* methods to convert between types.

As explained in the discussion on types, the rationale behind implicit conversions is that they are guaranteed to succeed and do not lose information during the conversion. Conversely, an explicit conversion should be required either when runtime circumstances will determine whether the conversion will succeed or if information may be lost during the conversion.

In this example, we define conversions between our musical Note type and a double (which represents the frequency in hertz of that note):

```
...
// Convert to hertz
public static implicit operator double (Note x)
{
  return 440 * Math.Pow (2,(double) x.value / 12 );
}

// Convert from hertz (accurate to nearest semitone)
public static explicit operator Note (double x)
{
  return new Note ((int) (0.5 + 12 * (Math.Log(x/440)
                / Math.Log(2)) ));
}
...

Note n =(Note)554.37;  // explicit conversion
double x = n;          // implicit conversion
```

Following our own guidelines, the example might be better implemented with a ToFrequency (and a static FromFrequency) method, not implicit and explicit operators.

Extension Methods (C# 3.0)

Extension methods allow an existing type to be extended with new methods, without altering the definition of the original type. An extension method is a static method of a static class, where the this modifier is applied to the first parameter. The type of the first parameter will be the type that is extended. For example:

```
public static class StringHelper
{
  public static bool IsCapitalized (this string s)
  {
    if (string.IsNullOrEmpty (s)) return false;
    return char.IsUpper (s[0]);
  }
}
```

The IsCapitalized extension method can be called as though it were an instance method on a string, as follows:

```
Console.Write ("Perth".IsCapitalized( ));
```

An extension method call, when compiled, is translated back into an ordinary static method call:

```
Console.Write (StringHelper.IsCapitalized ("Perth"));
```

Interfaces can be extended, too:

```
public static T First<T> (this IEnumerable<T> sequence)
{
  foreach (T element in sequence)
    return element;
  throw new InvalidOperationException ("No elements!");
}
...
Console.WriteLine ("Seattle".First( ));   // S
```

Extension Method Chaining

Extension methods, like instance methods, provide a tidy way to chain functions. Consider the following two functions:

```
public static class StringHelper
{
  public static string Pluralize (this string s) {...}
  public static string Capitalize (this string s) {...}
}
```

x and y are equivalent and both evaluate to "Sausages", but x uses extension methods, whereas y uses static methods:

```
string x = "sausage".Pluralize().Capitalize();

string y = StringHelper.Capitalize
           (StringHelper.Pluralize ("sausage"));
```

Ambiguity and Resolution

Namespaces

An extension method cannot be accessed unless the namespace is in scope (typically imported with a using statement).

Extension methods versus instance methods

Any compatible instance method will always take precedence over an extension method. In the following example, Test's Foo method will always take precedence—even when called with an argument x of type int:

```
class Test
{
  public void Foo (object x) { }    // This method
}                                   // always wins

static class Extensions
{
  public static void Foo (this Test t, int x) { }
}
```

The only way to call the extension method in this case is via normal static syntax; in other words, Extensions.Foo(...).

Extension methods versus extension methods

If two extension methods have the same signature, the extension method must be called as an ordinary static method to disambiguate the method to call. If one extension method has more specific arguments, however, the more specific method takes precedence.

To illustrate, consider the following two classes:

```
static class StringHelper
{
  public static bool IsCapitalized (this string s) {...}
}
static class ObjectHelper
{
  public static bool IsCapitalized (this object s) {...}
}
```

The following code calls StringHelper's IsCapitalized method:

```
bool test1 = "Perth".IsCapitalized();
```

To call ObjectHelper's IsCapitalized method, we explicitly must specify it:

```
bool test2 = (ObjectHelper.IsCapitalized ("Perth"));
```

Anonymous Types (C# 3.0)

An anonymous type is a simple class created on the fly to store a set of values. To create an anonymous type, use the new keyword followed by an object initializer, specifying the properties and values the type will contain. For example:

```
var dude = new { Name = "Bob", Age = 1 };
```

The compiler resolves this by writing a private nested type with read-only properties for Name (type string) and Age (type int). You must use the var keyword to reference an anonymous type, because the type's name is compiler-generated.

The property name of an anonymous type can be inferred from an expression that is itself an identifier. For example:

```
int Age = 1;
var dude = new { Name = "Bob", Age };
```

is equivalent to:

```
var dude = new { Name = "Bob", Age = Age };
```

Anonymous types are used primarily when writing LINQ queries.

LINQ (C# 3.0)

LINQ allows you to write structured type-safe queries over local object collections and remote data sources. LINQ is a new feature of C# 3.0 and .NET Framework 3.5.

LINQ lets you query any collection implementing IEnumerable<>, whether an array, list, XML DOM, or remote data source (such as a table in SQL Server). LINQ offers the benefits of both compile-time type checking and dynamic query composition.

NOTE

A good way to experiment with LINQ is to download LINQPad at *www.linqpad.net*. LINQPad lets you interactively query local collections and SQL databases in LINQ without any setup.

LINQ Fundamentals

The basic units of data in LINQ are *sequences* and *elements*. A sequence is any object that implements the generic IEnumerable interface and an element is each item in the sequence. In the following example, names is a sequence, and Tom, Dick, and Harry are elements:

```
string[] names = { "Tom", "Dick", "Harry" };
```

A sequence such as this we call a *local sequence* because it represents a local collection of objects in memory.

A *query operator* is a method that transforms a sequence. A typical query operator accepts an *input sequence* and emits a transformed *output sequence*. In the Enumerable class in System.Linq, there are around 40 query operators; all implemented as static extension methods. These are called standard query operators.

NOTE

LINQ also supports sequences that can be dynamically fed from a remote data source such as a SQL Server. These sequences additionally implement the IQueryable<> interface and are supported through a matching set of standard query operators in the Queryable class.

A simple query

A query is an expression that transforms sequences with one or more query operators. The simplest query comprises one input sequence and one operator. For instance, we can apply the Where operator on a simple array to extract those whose length is at least four characters as follows:

```
string[] names = { "Tom", "Dick", "Harry" };

IEnumerable<string> filteredNames =
  System.Linq.Enumerable.Where (
    names, n => n.Length >= 4);
```

```
foreach (string n in filteredNames)
  Console.Write (n + "|");            // Dick|Harry|
```

Because the standard query operators are implemented as extension methods, we can call Where directly on names—as though it were an instance method:

```
IEnumerable<string> filteredNames =
  names.Where (n => n.Length >= 4);
```

(For this to compile, you must import the System.Linq namespace with a using directive.) The Where method in System.Linq.Enumerable has the following signature:

```
static IEnumerable<TSource> Where<TSource> (
  this IEnumerable<TSource> source,
  Func<TSource,bool> predicate)
```

source is the *input sequence*; predicate is a delegate that is invoked on each input *element*. Where method includes all elements in the *output sequence*, for which the delegate returns true. Internally, it's implemented with an iterator—here is its source code:

```
foreach (TSource element in source)
  if (predicate (element))
    yield return element;
```

Projecting

Another fundamental query operator is the Select method. This transforms (*projects*) each element in the input sequence with a given lambda expression:

```
string[] names = { "Tom", "Dick", "Harry" };

IEnumerable<string> upperNames =
  names.Select (n => n.ToUpper());

foreach (string n in upperNames)
  Console.Write (n + "|");        // TOM|DICK|HARRY|
```

A query can project into an anonymous type:

```
var query = names.Select (n => new {
                                    Name = n,
                                    Length = n.Length
                                   });
```

```
foreach (var row in query)
  Console.WriteLine (row);
```

Here's the result:

```
{ Name = Tom, Length = 3 }
{ Name = Dick, Length = 4 }
{ Name = Harry, Length = 5 }
```

Take and Skip

The original ordering of elements within an input sequence is significant in LINQ. Some query operators rely on this behavior, such as Take, Skip, and Reverse. The Take operator outputs the first x elements, discarding the rest:

```
int[] numbers  = { 10, 9, 8, 7, 6 };
IEnumerable<int> firstThree = numbers.Take (3);
// firstThree is { 10, 9, 8 }
```

The Skip operator ignores the first x elements, and outputs the rest:

```
IEnumerable<int> lastTwo = numbers.Skip (3);
// lastTwo is { 7, 6 }
```

Element operators

Not all query operators return a sequence. The *element* operators extract one element from the input sequence; examples are First, Last, Single, and ElementAt:

```
int[] numbers  = { 10, 9, 8, 7, 6 };
int firstNumber  = numbers.First();       // 10
int lastNumber   = numbers.Last();        // 6
int secondNumber = numbers.ElementAt (2); // 8

int firstOddNumber = numbers.First (n => n % 2 == 1);
// 9
```

All of these operators throw an exception if no elements are present. To get a null/empty return value instead of an exception, use FirstOrDefault, LastOrDefault, SingleOrDefault, or ElementAtOrDefault.

The Single and SingleOrDefault methods are equivalent to First and FirstOrDefault except that they throw an exception if there's more than one match. This behavior is useful in LINQ to SQL queries, when retrieving a row by primary key.

Aggregation operators

The *aggregation* operators return a scalar value, usually of numeric type. The most commonly used aggregation operators are Count, Min, Max, and Average:

```
int[] numbers    = { 10, 9, 8, 7, 6 };
int count        = numbers.Count();        // 5
int min          = numbers.Min();          // 6
int max          = numbers.Max();          // 10
double avg       = numbers.Average();      // 8
```

Count accepts an optional predicate, which indicates whether to include a given element. The following counts all even numbers:

```
int evenNums = numbers.Count (n => n % 2 == 0);   // 3
```

The Min, Max, and Average operators accept an optional argument that transforms each element before it is aggregated:

```
int maxRemainderAfterDivBy5 = numbers.Max (n % 5);  // 4
```

The following calculates the root-mean-square of numbers:

```
double rms = Math.Sqrt (numbers.Average (n => n * n));
```

Quantifiers

The *quantifiers* return a bool value. The quantifiers are Contains, Any, All, and SequenceEquals (which compares two sequences):

```
int[] numbers = { 10, 9, 8, 7, 6 };

bool hasTheNumberNine = numbers.Contains (9);       // true
bool hasMoreThanZeroElements = numbers.Any();       // true
bool hasOddNum = numbers.Any (n => n % 2 == 1);     // true
bool allOddNums = numbers.All (n => n % 2 == 1);    // false
```

Set operators

The *set* operators accept two same-typed input sequences.
Concat appends one sequence to another; Union does the
same but with duplicates removed:

```
int[] seq1 = { 1, 2, 3 }, seq2 = { 3, 4, 5 };

IEnumerable<int>
  concat = seq1.Concat (seq2),   // { 1, 2, 3, 3, 4, 5 }
  union  = seq1.Union  (seq2),   // { 1, 2, 3, 4, 5 }
```

The other two operators in this category are Intersect and
Except:

```
IEnumerable<int>
  commonality = seq1.Intersect (seq2),   // { 3 }
  difference1 = seq1.Except    (seq2),   // { 1, 2 }
  difference2 = seq2.Except    (seq1);   // { 4, 5 }
```

Deferred Execution

An important feature of many query operators is that they
execute not when constructed, but when *enumerated* (in
other words, when MoveNext is called on its enumerator).
Consider the following query:

```
var numbers = new List<int> { 1 };
numbers.Add (1);

IEnumerable<int> query = numbers.Select (n => n * 10);
numbers.Add (2);    // Sneak in an extra element

foreach (int n in query)
  Console.Write (n + "|");          // 10|20|
```

The extra number that we sneaked into the list *after* constructing the query is included in the result because it's not
until the foreach statement runs that any filtering or sorting
takes place. This is called *deferred* or *lazy* evaluation.
Deferred execution decouples query *construction* from query
execution, allowing you to construct a query in several steps,
as well as making LINQ to SQL queries possible. All standard query operators provide deferred execution, with the
following exceptions:

- Operators that return a single element or scalar value (the *element operators*, *aggregation operators*, and *quantifiers*)
- The following *conversion* operators:

    ```
    ToArray, ToList, ToDictionary, ToLookup
    ```

The conversion operators are useful, in part, because they defeat lazy evaluation. This can be useful when:

- You want to "freeze" or cache the results at a certain point in time.
- You want to avoid reexecuting a computationally intensive query, or a query with a remote data source such as a LINQ to SQL table. (A side effect of lazy evaluation is the query gets reevaluated should you later reenumerate it.)

The following example illustrates the ToList operator:

```
var numbers = new List<int>() { 1, 2 };

List<int> timesTen = numbers
  .Select (n => n * 10)
  .ToList();    // Executes immediately into a List<int>

numbers.Clear();
Console.WriteLine (timesTen.Count);    // Still 2
```

WARNING

Subqueries provide another level of indirection. Everything in a subquery is subject to deferred execution—including aggregation and conversion methods—because the subquery is itself executed only lazily upon demand. Assuming names is a string array, a subquery looks like this:

```
names.Where (
  n => n.Length ==
    names.Min (n2 => n2.Length)
  )
```

Standard Query Operators

The standard query operators (as implemented in the System. Linq.Enumerable class) can be divided into 12 categories, as summarized in Table 2.

Table 2. Query operator categories

Category	Description	Deferred execution?
Filtering	Returns a subset of elements that satisfy a given condition	Yes
Projecting	Transforms each element with a lambda function, optionally expanding subsequences	Yes
Joining	Meshes elements of one collection with another, using a time-efficient lookup strategy	Yes
Ordering	Returns a reordering of a sequence	Yes
Grouping	Groups a sequence into subsequences	Yes
Set	Accepts two same-typed sequences, and returns their commonality, sum, or difference	Yes
Element	Picks a single element from a sequence	No
Aggregation	Performs a computation over a sequence, returning a scalar value (typically a number)	No
Quantifiers	Performs a computation over a sequence, returning true or false	No
Conversion: Import	Converts a nongeneric sequence to a (queryable) generic sequence	Yes
Conversion: Export	Converts a sequence to an array, list, dictionary or lookup, forcing immediate evaluation	No
Generation	Manufactures a simple sequence	Yes

Tables 3–14 summarize each of the query operators. The operators shown in bold have special support in C# 3.0 (see the upcoming "Query Syntax" section).

Table 3. Filtering operators

Method	Description
Where	Returns a subset of elements that satisfy a given condition
Take	Returns the first x elements, and discards the rest
Skip	Ignores the first x elements, and returns the rest
TakeWhile	Emits elements from the input sequence until the given predicate is true
SkipWhile	Ignores elements from the input sequence until the given predicate is true, and then emits the rest
Distinct	Returns a collection that excludes duplicates

Table 4. Projection operators

Method	Description
Select	Transforms each input element with a given lambda expression
SelectMany	Transforms each input element, then flattens and concatenates the resultant subsequences

Table 5. Joining operators

Method	Description
Join	Applies a lookup strategy to match elements from two collections, emitting a flat result set
GroupJoin	As above, but emits a *hierarchical* result set

Table 6. Ordering operators

Method	Description
OrderBy, ThenBy	Returns the elements sorted in ascending order
OrderByDescending, ThenByDescending	Returns the elements sorted in descending order
Reverse	Returns the elements in reverse order

Table 7. Grouping operators

Method	Description
GroupBy	Groups a sequence into subsequences

Table 8. Set operators

Method	Description
Concat	Concatenates two sequences
Union	Concatenates two sequences, removing duplicates
Intersect	Returns elements present in both sequences
Except	Returns elements present in the first, but not the second sequence

Table 9. Element operators

Method	Description
First, FirstOrDefault	Returns the first element in the sequence, or the first element satisfying a given predicate
Last, LastOrDefault	Returns the last element in the sequence, or the last element satisfying a given predicate
Single, SingleOrDefault	Equivalent to First/FirstOrDefault, but throws an exception if there is more than one match
ElementAt, ElementAtOrDefault	Returns the element at the specified position
DefaultIfEmpty	Returns null or default(TSource) if the sequence has no elements

Table 10. Aggregation operators

Method	Description
Count, LongCount	Returns the total number of elements in the input sequence, or the number of elements satisfying a given predicate
Min, Max	Returns the smallest or largest element in the sequence
Sum, Average	Calculates a numeric sum or average over elements in the sequence
Aggregate	Performs a custom aggregation

Table 11. Qualifiers

Method	Description
Contains	Returns true if the input sequence contains the given element
Any	Returns true if any elements satisfy the given predicate
All	Returns true if all elements satisfy the given predicate
SequenceEqual	Returns true if the second sequence has identical elements to the input sequence

Table 12. Conversion operators (import)

Method	Description
OfType	Converts IEnumerable to IEnumerable<T>, discarding wrongly typed elements
Cast	Converts IEnumerable to IEnumerable<T>, throwing an exception if there are any wrongly typed elements

Table 13. Table conversion operators (export)

Method	Description
ToArray	Converts IEnumerable<T> to T[]
ToList	Converts IEnumerable<T> to List<T>
ToDictionary	Converts IEnumerable<T> to Dictionary<TKey,TValue>
ToLookup	Converts IEnumerable<T> to ILookup<TKey,TElement>
AsEnumerable	Downcasts to IEnumerable<T>
AsQueryable	Casts or converts to IQueryable<T>

Table 14. Generation operators

Method	Description
Empty	Creates an empty sequence
Repeat	Creates a sequence of repeating elements
Range	Creates a sequence of integers

Chaining Query Operators

To build more complex queries, you chain query operators together. For example, the following query extracts all strings containing the letter *a*, sorts them by length, and then converts the results to uppercase:

```
string[] names = { "Tom","Dick","Harry","Mary","Jay" };

IEnumerable<string> query = names
  .Where   (n => n.Contains ("a"))
  .OrderBy (n => n.Length)
  .Select  (n => n.ToUpper());

foreach (string name in query)
  Console.Write (name + "|");

// RESULT: JAY|MARY|HARRY|
```

Where, OrderBy, and Select are all standard query operators that resolve to extension methods in the Enumerable class. The Where operator emits a filtered version of the input sequence; OrderBy emits a sorted version of its input sequence; Select emits a sequence where each input element is transformed or *projected* with a given lambda expression (n.ToUpper(), in this case). Data flows from left to right through the chain of operators, so the data is first filtered, then sorted, then projected. The end result resembles a production line of conveyor belts, as illustrated in Figure 6.

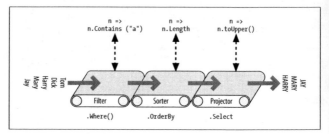

Figure 6. Chaining query operators

Deferred execution is honored throughout with operators, so no filtering, sorting, or projecting takes place until the query is actually enumerated.

Query Syntax

C# 3.0 provides special language support for writing queries, called *query comprehension syntax* or *query syntax*. Here's the preceding query expressed in query syntax:

```
using System.Linq;
...

string[] names = { "Tom","Dick","Harry","Mary","Jay" };

IEnumerable<string> query =
  from n in names
  where n.Contains ("a")
  orderby n.Length
  select n.ToUpper( );
```

A comprehension query always starts with a from clause and ends with either a select or group clause. The from clause declares an *iteration variable* (in this case, n) which you can think of as traversing the input collection—rather like foreach. Figure 7 illustrates the complete syntax.

NOTE

If you're familiar with SQL, LINQ's query syntax—with the from clause first and the select clause last—might look bizarre. Query syntax is actually more logical because the clauses appear *in the order they're executed*. This allows Visual Studio to prompt you with Intellisense as you type, as well as simplifying the scoping rules for subqueries.

The compiler processes comprehension queries by translating them to lambda syntax. It does this in a fairly mechanical fashion—much like it translates foreach statements into calls to GetEnumerator and MoveNext:

```
IEnumerable<string> query = names
    .Where   (n => n.Contains ("a"))
    .OrderBy (n => n.Length)
    .Select  (n => n.ToUpper());.
```

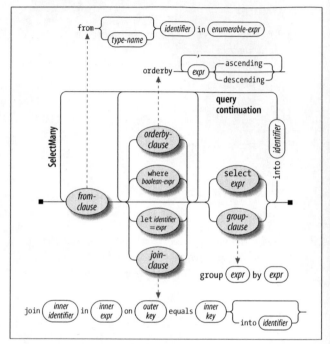

Figure 7. Query comprehension syntax

The Where, OrderBy, and Select operators then resolve using the same rules that would apply if the query were written in lambda syntax. In this case, they bind to extension methods in the Enumerable class (assuming you've imported the System.Linq namespace) because names implements IEnumerable<string>. The compiler doesn't specifically favor the Enumerable class, however, when translating query syntax. You can think of the compiler as mechanically injecting the words "Where," "OrderBy," and "Select" into the statement, and then compiling it as though you'd typed the method names yourself. This offers flexibility in how they resolve—the operators in LINQ to SQL queries, for instance, bind instead to the extension methods in the `Queryable` class.

Query syntax versus lambda syntax

Query syntax and lambda syntax each have advantages.

Query syntax supports only a small subset of query operators, namely:

```
Where, Select, SelectMany
OrderBy, ThenBy, OrderByDescending, ThenByDescending
GroupBy, Join, GroupJoin
```

For queries that use other operators, you must either write entirely in lambda syntax or construct mixed-syntax queries, for instance:

```
string[] names = { "Tom","Dick","Harry","Mary","Jay" };

IEnumerable<string> query =
  from   n in names
  where  n.Length == names.Min (n2 => n2.Length)
  select n;
```

This query returns names whose length matches that of the shortest ("Tom" and "Jay"). The subquery (in bold) calculates the minimum length of each name, and evaluates to 3. We have to use lambda syntax for the subquery because the `Min` operator has no support in query syntax. We can, however, still use query syntax for the outer query.

The main advantage of query syntax is that it can radically simplify queries that involve the following:

- A `let` clause for introducing a new variable alongside the iteration variable
- Multiple generators (`SelectMany`) followed by an outer iteration variable reference
- A `Join` or `GroupJoin` equivalent, followed by an outer iteration variable reference

The let Keyword

The let keyword introduces a new variable alongside the iteration variable. For instance, suppose we want to list all names whose length without vowels is greater than two characters:

```
string[] names = { "Tom","Dick","Harry","Mary","Jay" };

IEnumerable<string> query =
  from n in names
  let vowelless = Regex.Replace (n, "[aeiou]", "")
  where vowelless.Length > 2
  orderby vowelless
  select n + " - " + vowelless;
```

The output from enumerating this query is:

```
Dick - Dck
Harry - Hrry
Mary - Mry
```

The let clause performs a calculation on each element, without losing the original element. In our query, the subsequent clauses (where, orderby, and select) have access to both n and vowelless. Queries can include any multiple let clauses, and they can be interspersed with additional where and join clauses.

The compiler translates the let keyword by projecting into a temporary anonymous type that contains both the original and transformed elements:

```
IEnumerable<string> query = names
 .Select (n =>  new
   {
     n = n,
     vowelless = Regex.Replace (n, "[aeiou]", "")
   }
 )
 .Where (temp0 => (temp0.vowelless.Length > 2))
 .OrderBy (temp0 => temp0.vowelless)
 .Select (temp0 => ((temp0.n + " - ") + temp0.vowelless))
```

Query Continuations

If you want to add clauses *after* a select or group clause, you must use the into keyword to "continue" the query. For instance:

```
from c in "The quick brown tiger".Split()
select c.ToUpper()
into upper
where upper.StartsWith ("T")
select upper

// RESULT: "THE", "TIGER"
```

Following an into clause, the previous iteration variable is out of scope.

The compiler translates queries with an into keyword simply into a longer chain of lambda operators:

```
"The quick brown tiger".Split()
  .Select (c => c.ToUpper())
  .Where (upper => upper.StartsWith ("T"))
```

(It omits the final Select(upper=>upper), as it's redundant.)

Multiple Generators

A query can include multiple generators (from clauses). For example:

```
int[] numbers = { 1, 2, 3 };
string[] letters = { "a", "b" };

IEnumerable<string> query = from n in numbers
                            from l in letters
                            select n.ToString() + l;
```

The result is a cross product, rather like you'd get with nested foreach loops:

```
"1a", "1b", "2a", "2b", "3a", "3b"
```

When there's more than one from clause in a query, the compiler emits a call to SelectMany:

```
IEnumerable<string> query = numbers.SelectMany (
  n => letters,
  (n, l) => (n.ToString( ) + l));
```

SelectMany performs nested looping. It enumerates every element in the source collection (numbers), transforming each element with the first lambda expression (letters). This generates a sequence of *subsequences*, which it then enumerates. The final output elements are determined by the second lambda expression (n.ToString( )+l).

If you subsequently apply a where clause, you can filter the cross product and project a result akin to a *join*:

```
string[] players = { "Tom", "Jay", "Mary" };

IEnumerable<string> query =
  from name1 in players
  from name2 in players
  where name1.CompareTo (name2) < 0
  orderby name1, name2
  select name1 + " vs " + name2;

RESULT: { "Jay vs Mary", "Jay vs Tom", "Mary vs Tom" }
```

The translation of this query into lambda syntax is considerably more complex, requiring a temporary anonymous projection. The ability to perform this translation automatically is one of the key benefits of query syntax.

The expression in the second generator is allowed to use the first iteration variable:

```
string[] fullNames =
  { "Anne Williams", "John Fred Smith", "Sue Green" };

IEnumerable<string> query =
  from fullName in fullNames
  from name in fullName.Split( )
  select name + " came from " + fullName;
```

```
Anne came from Anne Williams
Williams came from Anne Williams
John came from John Fred Smith
```

This works because the expression `fullName.Split` emits a *sequence* (an array of strings).

Multiple generators are used extensively in LINQ to SQL queries to flatten parent-child relationships and to perform manual joins.

Joining

LINQ provides *joining* operators for performing keyed lookup-based joins. The joining operators support only a subset of the functionality you get with multiple generators/`SelectMany`, but they are more performant with local queries because they use a hashtable-based lookup strategy rather than performing nested loops. (With LINQ to SQL queries, the joining operators have no advantage over multiple generators.)

The joining operators support equijoins only (i.e., the joining condition must use the equality operator). There are two methods: `Join` and `GroupJoin`. `Join` emits a flat result set, whereas `GroupJoin` emits a hierarchical result set.

The syntax for a flat join is:

```
from outer-var in outer-sequence
join inner-var in inner-sequence
  on outer-key expr equals inner-key-expr
```

For example, given the following collections:

```
var customers = new[]
{
    new { ID = 1, Name = "Tom" },
    new { ID = 2, Name = "Dick" },
    new { ID = 3, Name = "Harry" }
};
var purchases = new[]
{
```

```
        new { CustomerID = 1, Product = "House" },
        new { CustomerID = 2, Product = "Boat" },
        new { CustomerID = 2, Product = "Car" },
        new { CustomerID = 3, Product = "Holiday" }
};
```

we could perform a join as follows:

```
IEnumerable<string> query =
    from c in customers
    join p in purchases on c.ID equals p.CustomerID
    select c.Name + " bought a " + p.Product;
```

The compiler translates this to:

```
customers.Join (                    // outer collection
    purchases,                      // inner collection
    c => c.ID,                      // outer key selector
    p => p.CustomerID,              // inner key selector
    (c, p) =>                       // result selector
        c.Name + " bought a " + p.Product
);
```

Here's the result:

```
Tom bought a House
Dick bought a Boat
Dick bought a Car
Harry bought a Holiday
```

With local sequences, the join operators are more efficient at processing large collections than SelectMany because they first preload the inner sequence into a keyed hashtable-based lookup. With a LINQ to SQL query, however, you could achieve the same result equally efficiently as follows:

```
from c in customers
from p in purchases
where c.ID == p.CustomerID
select c.Name + " bought a " + p.Product;
```

GroupJoin

GroupJoin does the same work as Join, but instead of yielding a flat result, it yields a hierarchical result, grouped by each outer element.

The comprehension syntax for GroupJoin is the same as for Join, but is followed by the into keyword. Here's a basic example, using the customers and purchases collections we set up in the previous section:

```
IEnumerable<IEnumerable<Purchase>> query =
  from c in customers
  join p in purchases on c.ID equals p.CustomerID
  into custPurchases
  select custPurchases;   // custPurchases is a sequence
```

NOTE

An into clause translates to GroupJoin only when it appears directly after a join clause. After a select or group clause it means *query continuation*. The two uses of the into keyword are quite different, although they have one feature in common: they both introduce a new query variable.

The result is a sequence of sequences that we could enumerate as follows:

```
foreach (IEnumerable<Purchase> purchaseSequence in query)
  foreach (Purchase p in purchaseSequence)
    Console.WriteLine (p.Description);
```

This isn't very useful, however, because outerSeq has no reference to the outer customer. More commonly, you'd reference the outer iteration variable in the projection:

```
from c in customers
join p in purchases on c.ID equals p.CustomerID
into custPurchases
select new { CustName = c.Name, custPurchases };
```

We could obtain the same result (but less efficiently, for local queries) by projecting into an anonymous type that included a subquery:

```
from c in customers
select new
{
```

```
      CustName = c.Name,
      custPurchases =
        purchases.Where (p => c.ID == p.CustomerID)
    }
```

Ordering

The orderby keyword sorts a sequence. You can specify any number of expressions upon which to sort:

```
string[] names = { "Tom","Dick","Harry","Mary","Jay" };

IEnumerable<string> query = from n in names
                           orderby n.Length, n
                           select n;
```

This sorts first by length, then name, so the result is:

```
Jay, Tom, Dick, Mary, Harry
```

The compiler translates the first orderby expression to a call to OrderBy, and subsequent expressions to a call to ThenBy:

```
IEnumerable<string> query = names
  .OrderBy (n => n.Length)
  .ThenBy (n => n)
```

The ThenBy operator *refines* rather than *replaces* the previous sorting.

You can include the descending keyword after any of the orderby expressions:

```
orderby n.Length descending, n
```

This translates to the following:

```
.OrderByDescending (n => n.Length).ThenBy (n => n)
```

NOTE

The ordering operators return an extended type of IEnumerable<T> called IOrderedEnumerble<T>. This interface defines the extra functionality required by the ThenBy operators.

Grouping

GroupBy organizes a flat input sequence into sequences of *groups*. For example, the following groups a sequence of names by their length:

```
string[] names = { "Tom","Dick","Harry","Mary","Jay" };

var query = from name in names
            group name by name.Length;
```

The compiler translates this query into this:

```
IEnumerable<IGrouping<int,string>> query =
  names.GroupBy (name => name.Length);
```

Here's how to enumerate the result:

```
foreach (IGrouping<int,string> grouping in query)
{
  Console.Write ("\r\n Length=" + grouping.Key + ":");
  foreach (string name in grouping)
    Console.Write (" " + name);
}

 Length=3: Tom Jay
 Length=4: Dick Mary
 Length=5: Harry
```

Enumerable.GroupBy works by reading the input elements into a temporary dictionary of lists so that all elements with the same key end up in the same sublist. It then emits a sequence of *groupings*. A grouping is a sequence with a Key property:

```
public interface IGrouping <TKey,TElement>
  : IEnumerable<TElement>, IEnumerable
{
  // Key applies to the subsequence as a whole
  TKey Key { get; }
}
```

By default, the elements in each grouping are untransformed input elements unless you specify an elementSelector argument. The following projects each input element to uppercase:

```
from name in names
group name.ToUpper( ) by name.Length
```

which translates to this:

```
names.GroupBy (
    name => name.Length,
    name => name.ToUpper( ) )
```

The subcollections are not emitted in order of key. GroupBy does no *sorting* (in fact, it preserves the original ordering.) To sort, you must add an OrderBy operator (which means first adding an into clause because group by ordinarily ends a query):

```
from name in names
group name.ToUpper( ) by name.Length
into grouping
orderby grouping.Key
select grouping
```

Query continuations are often used in a group by query. The next query filters out groups that have exactly two matches in them:

```
from name in names
group name.ToUpper( ) by name.Length
into grouping
where grouping.Count( ) == 2
select grouping
```

NOTE

A where after a group by is equivalent to HAVING in SQL. It applies to each subsequence or grouping as a whole rather than the individual elements.

OfType and Cast

OfType and Cast accept a nongeneric IEnumerable collection and emit a generic IEnumerable<T> sequence that you can subsequently query:

```
var classicList = new System.Collections.ArrayList( );
classicList.AddRange ( new int[] { 3, 4, 5 } );
IEnumerable<int> sequence1 = classicList.Cast<int>( );
```

This is useful because it allows you to query collections written prior to C# 2.0 (when `IEnumerable<T>` was introduced), such as `ControlCollection` in `System.Windows.Forms`.

`Cast` and `OfType` differ in their behavior when encountering an input element that's of an incompatible type: `Cast` throws an exception, whereas `OfType` ignores the incompatible element.

The rules for element compatiblity follow those of C#'s `is` operator. Here's the internal implementation of `Cast`:

```
public static IEnumerable<TSource> Cast <TSource>
             (IEnumerable source)
{
  foreach (object element in source)
    yield return (TSource)element;
}
```

C# supports the `Cast` operator in query syntax. Simply insert the element type immediately after the `from` keyword:

```
from int x in classicList
...
```

This translates to the following:

```
from x in classicList.Cast <int>()
...
```

Attributes

You're already familiar with the notion of attributing code elements of a program with modifiers, such as `virtual` or `ref`. These constructs are built into the language. *Attributes* are an extensible mechanism for adding custom information to code elements (assemblies, types, members, return values, and parameters). This extensiblity is useful for services that integrate deeply into the type system, without requiring special keywords or constructs in the C# language.

A good scenario for attributes is *serialization*—the process of converting arbitrary objects to and from a particular format.

In this scenario, an attribute on a field can specify the translation between C#'s representation of the field and the format's representation of the field.

Attribute Classes

An attribute is defined by a class that inherits (directly or indirectly) from the abstract class `System.Attribute`. To attach an attribute to a code element, you specify the attribute's type name in square brackets, before the code element. For example, the following attaches the `ObsoleteAttribute` to the Foo class:

```
[ObsoleteAttribute]
public class Foo { ... }
```

This attribute is recognized by the compiler and will cause compiler warnings if a type or member marked obsolete is referenced. By convention, all attribute types end in the word "Attribute." C# recognizes this and allows you to omit the suffix when attaching an attribute:

```
[Obsolete]
public class Foo { ... }
```

`ObsoleteAttribute` is a type declared in the `System` namespace as follows (simplified for brevity):

```
public sealed class ObsoleteAttribute : Attribute
{ ... }
```

Named and Positional Parameters

Attributes may have parameters. In the following example, we apply the `XmlElement` attribute to a class. The `XmlElement` attribute tells the `System.Xml.Linq` model how an object is represented in XML. The `XmlElement` attribute accepts several *attribute parameters*. The following attribute maps the `CustomerEntity` class to an XML element named `Customer`, belonging to the `http://oreilly.com` namespace:

```
[XmlElement ("Customer", Namespace="http://blah")]
public class CustomerEntity { ... }
```

Attribute parameters fall into one of two categories: positional and named. In the preceding example, the first argument is a positional parameter; the second is a named parameter. Positional parameters correspond to parameters of the attribute type's public constructors. Named parameters correspond to public fields or public properties on the attribute type.

When specifying an attribute, you must include positional parameters that correspond to one of the attribute's constructors. Named parameters are optional.

Attribute Targets

Implicitly, the target of an attribute is the code element it immediately precedes, which is typically a type or type member. You can also attach attributes, however, to an assembly. This requires that you explicitly specify the attribute's target.

Here is an example of using the CLSCompliant attribute to specify CLS compliance for an entire assembly:

```
[assembly:CLSCompliant(true)]
```

Specifying Multiple Attributes

Multiple attributes can be specified for a single code element. Each attribute can be listed either within the same pair of square brackets (separated by a comma), or in separate pairs of square brackets (or a combination of the two).

The following three examples are semantically identical:

```
[Serializable, Obsolete, CLSCompliant(false)]
public class Bar {...}

[Serializable] [Obsolete] [CLSCompliant(false)]
public class Bar {...}

[Serializable, Obsolete]
[CLSCompliant(false)]
public class Bar {...}
```

Writing Custom Attributes

You can define your own by subclassing System.Attribute. For example, we could use the following custom attribute for flagging a method for unit testing:

```
[AttributeUsage (AttributeTargets.Method)]
public sealed class TestAttribute : Attribute
{
  public int     Repetitions;
  public string  FailureMessage;

  public TestAttribute () : this (1) { }
  public TestAttribute (int repetitions)
  {
    Repetitions = repetitions;
  }
}
```

Here's how we could apply the attribute:

```
class Foo
{
  [Test]
  public void Method1() { ... }

  [Test(20)]
  public void Method2() { ... }

  [Test(20, FailureMessage="Debugging Time!")]
  public void Method3() { ... }
}
```

AttributeUsage is itself an attribute that indicates the construct (or combination of constructs) that the custom attribute can be applied to. The AttributeTargets enum includes such members as Class, Method, Parameter, Constructor (and All, which combines all targets).

Retrieving Attributes at Runtime

There are two standard ways to retrieve attributes at runtime:

- Call `GetCustomAttributes` on any `Type` or `MemberInfo` object.
- Call `Attribute.GetCustomAttribute` or `Attribute.GetCustomAttributes`.

These latter two methods are overloaded to accept any reflection object that corresponds to a valid attribute target (`Type`, `Assembly`, `Module`, `MemberInfo`, or `ParameterInfo`).

Here's how we can enumerate each method in the preceding `Foo` class that has a `TestAttribute`:

```
foreach (MethodInfo mi in typeof (Foo).GetMethods( ))
{
  TestAttribute att = (TestAttribute)
    Attribute.GetCustomAttribute
    (mi, typeof (TestAttribute));

  if (att != null)
    Console.WriteLine (
      "Method {0} will be tested; reps={1}; msg={2}",
      mi.Name, att.Repetitions, att.FailureMessage);
}
```

Here's the output:

```
Method Method1 will be tested; reps=1; msg=
Method Method2 will be tested; reps=20; msg=
Method Method3 will be tested; reps=20; msg=Debugging
Time!
```

Unsafe Code and Pointers

C# supports direct memory manipulation via pointers within blocks of code marked unsafe and compiled with the /unsafe compiler option. Pointer types are primarily useful for interoperability with C APIs, but they may also be used for accessing memory outside the managed heap or for performance-critical hotspots.

Pointer Basics

For every value type or pointer type *V*, there is a corresponding pointer type *V**. A pointer instance holds the address of a value. This is considered to be of type *V*, but pointer types can be (unsafely) cast to any other pointer type.

The main pointer operators are listed below.

Operator	Meaning
&	The *address-of* operator returns a pointer to the address of a value.
*	The *dereference* operator returns the value at the address of a pointer.
->	The *pointer-to-member* operator is a syntactic shortcut, in which x->y is equivalent to (*x).y.

Unsafe Code

By marking a type, type member, or statement block with the unsafe keyword, you're permitted to use pointer types and perform C++ style pointer operations on memory within that scope. Here is an example of using pointers to quickly process a bitmap:

```
unsafe void RedFilter(int[,] bitmap)
{
  int length = bitmap.Length;
  fixed (int* b = bitmap)
  {
    int* p = b;
    for(int i = 0; i < length; i++)
      *p++ &= 0xFF;
  }
}
```

Unsafe code can run faster than a corresponding safe implementation. In this case, the code would have required a nested loop with array indexing and bounds checking. An unsafe C# method may also be faster than calling an external C function because there is no overhead associated with leaving the managed execution environment.

The fixed Statement

The fixed statement is required to pin a managed object, such as the bitmap in the previous example. During the execution of a program, many objects are allocated and deallocated from the heap. To avoid unnecessary waste or fragmentation of memory, the garbage collector moves objects around. Pointing to an object is futile if its address could change while referencing it, so the fixed statement tells the garbage collector to "pin" the object and not move it around. This may have an impact on the efficiency of the runtime, so fixed blocks should be used only briefly, and heap allocation should be avoided within the fixed block.

Within a fixed statement, you can get a pointer to any value type, an array of value types, or a string. In the case of arrays and strings, the pointer will actually point to the first element, which is a value type.

Value types declared inline within reference types require the reference type to be pinned, as follows:

```
class Test
{
  int x;
  static void Main()
  {
    Test test = new Test();
    unsafe
    {
      fixed (int* p = &test.x)   // pins test
      {
        *p = 9;
      }
      System.Console.WriteLine (test.x);
    }
  }
}
```

The Pointer-to-Member Operator

In addition to the & and * operators, C# also provides the C++ style -> operator, which can be used on structs:

```
struct Test
{
  int x;
  unsafe static void Main()
  {
    Test test = new Test();
    Test* p = &test;
    p->x = 9;
    System.Console.WriteLine (test.x);
  }
}
```

Arrays

The stackalloc keyword

Memory can be allocated in a block on the stack explicitly using the stackalloc keyword. Because it is allocated on the stack, its lifetime is limited to the execution of the method, just as with any other local variable. The block may use the [] operator to index into memory.

```
int* a = stackalloc int [10];
for (int i = 0; i < 10; ++i)
  Console.WriteLine(a[i]); // print raw memory
```

Fixed-size buffers

Memory can be allocated in a block within a struct using the fixed keyword:

```
unsafe struct UnsafeUnicodeString
{
  public short Length;
  public fixed byte Buffer[30];
}

unsafe class UnsafeClass
{
```

```
    private UnsafeUnicodeString uus;
    public UnsafeClass (string s)
    {
      uus.Length = (short)s.Length;
      fixed (byte* p = uus.Buffer)
        for (int i = 0; i < s.Length; i++)
          p[i] = (byte)s[i];
    }
  }

  class Test
  {
    static void Main( )
      { new UnsafeClass ("Christian Troy"); }
  }
```

The `fixed` keyword is also used in this example to pin the object on the heap that contains the buffer (which will be the instance of `UnsafeClass`).

void*

Rather than pointing to a specific value type, a pointer may make no assumptions about the type of the underlying data. This approach is useful for functions that deal with raw memory. An implicit conversion exists from any pointer type to `void*`. A `void*` cannot be dereferenced and arithmetic operations cannot be performed on void pointers. For example:

```
  class Test
  {
    unsafe static void Main( )
    {
      short[ ] a = {1,1,2,3,5,8,13,21,34,55};
        fixed (short* p = a)
        {
          //sizeof returns size of value-type in bytes
          Zap (p, a.Length * sizeof (short));
        }
      foreach (short x in a)
        System.Console.WriteLine (x); // prints all zeros
    }
```

```
unsafe static void Zap (void* memory, int byteCount)
{
  byte* b = (byte*)memory;
    for (int i = 0; i < byteCount; i++)
      *b++ = 0;
}
}
```

Pointers to Unmanaged Code

Pointers are also useful for accessing data outside the managed heap (such as when interacting with C DLLs or COM), or when dealing with data not in the main memory (such as graphics memory or a storage medium on an embedded device).

Preprocessor Directives

Preprocessor directives supply the compiler with additional information about regions of code. The most common preprocessor directives are the conditional directives, which provide a way to include or exclude regions of code from compilation. For example:

```
#define DEBUG
class MyClass
{
  int x;
  void Foo( )
  {
    # if DEBUG
    Console.WriteLine("Testing: x = {0}", x);
    # endif
  }
  ...
}
```

In this class, the statement in Foo is compiled as conditionally dependent upon the presence of the DEBUG symbol. If we remove the DEBUG symbol, the statement is not compiled. Preprocessor symbols can be defined within a source file (as we have done), and they can be passed to the compiler with the /define: symbol command-line option.

With the #if and #elif directives, you can use the ||, &&, and ! operators to perform *or*, *and*, and *not* operations on multiple symbols. The following directive instructs the compiler to include the code that follows if the TESTMODE symbol is defined and the DEBUG symbol is not defined:

```
#if TESTMODE && !DEBUG
    ...
```

Bear in mind, however, that you're not building an ordinary C# expression, and the symbols upon which you operate have absolutely no connection to *variables*—static or otherwise.

The #error and #warning symbols prevent accidental misuse of conditional directives by making the compiler generate a warning or error given an undesirable set of compilation symbols.

Table 15 lists all preprocessor directives and their actions.

Table 15. Preprocessor directives

Preprocessor directive	Action
#define *symbol*	Defines *symbol*.
#undef *symbol*	Undefines *symbol*.
#if *symbol*	Conditionally compiles code.
#else	Executes code to subsequent #endif.
#elif *symbol*	Combines #else branch and #if test.
#endif	Ends conditional directives.
#warning *text*	*text* of the warning to appear in compiler output.
#error *text*	*text* of the error to appear in compiler output.
#line [*number* ["*file*"] | hidden]	*number* specifies the line in source code; *file* is the filename to appear in computer output; hidden instructs debuggers to skip over code from this point until the next #line directive.
#region *name*	Marks the beginning of an outline.
#end *region*	Ends an outline region.

Conditional Attributes

An attribute decorated with the Conditional attribute will be compiled only if a given preprocessor symbol is present, e.g.:

```
// file1.cs
#define DEBUG
using System;
using System.Diagnostics;

[Conditional("DEBUG")]
public class TestAttribute : Attribute {}

// file2.cs
#define DEBUG
[Test] class Foo
{
  [Test] string s;
}
```

The compiler will not incorporate the [Test] attributes if the DEBUG symbol is in scope for *file2.cs*.

Pragma Warning

The compiler generates a warning when it spots something in your code that seems unintentional. Unlike errors, warnings don't ordinarily prevent your application from compiling.

Compiler warnings can be extremely valuable in spotting bugs. Their usefulness, however, is undermined when you get an excessive number of them. In a large application, maintaining a good signal-to-noise ratio is essential if the "real" warnings are to get noticed.

To this effect, the compiler allows you to selectively suppress warnings with the #pragma warning directive. In this example, we instruct the compiler not to warn us about the field Message not being used:

```
public class Foo
{
  static void Main( ) { }
```

```
    #pragma warning disable 414
    static string Message = "Hello";
    #pragma warning restore 414
}
```

Omitting the number in the #pragma warning directive disables
or restores all warning codes. If you are thorough in applying
this directive, you can compile with the /warnaserror switch—
this tells the compiler to treat any residual warnings as errors.

XML Documentation

A *documentation comment* is a piece of embedded XML that
documents a type or member. A documentation comment
comes immediately before a type or member declaration, and
starts with three slashes:

```
/// <summary>Cancels a running query.</summary>
public void Cancel() { ... }
```

Multiline comments can be done either like this:

```
/// <summary>
/// Cancels a running query
/// </summary>
public void Cancel() { ... }
```

or this (notice the extra star at the start):

```
/**
    <summary> Cancels a running query. </summary>
*/
    public void Cancel() { ... }
```

If you compile with the /doc directive, the compiler extracts
and collates documentation comments into a single XML
file. This has two main uses:

- If placed in the same folder as the compiled assembly,
  Visual Studio automatically reads the XML file and uses
  the information to provide Intellisense member listings to
  consumers of that assembly.

- Third-party tools can transform an XML file into an
  HTML help file.

Standard XML Documentation Tags

Here are the standard XML tags that Visual Studio and documentation generators recognize:

`<summary>`

```
<summary>...</summary>
```

Indicates the tool tip that IntelliSense should display for the type or member. Typically a single phrase or sentence.

`<remarks>`

```
<remarks>...</remarks>
```

Additional text that describes the type or member. Documentation generators pick this up and merge it into the bulk of a type or member's description.

`<param>`

```
<param name="name">...</param>
```

Explains a parameter on a method.

`<returns>`

```
<returns>...</returns>
```

Explains the return value for a method.

`<exception>`

```
<exception [cref="type"]>...</exception>
```

Lists an exception that a method may throw (cref refers to the exception type).

`<permission>`

```
<permission [cref="type"]>...</permission>
```

Indicates an IPermission type required by the documented type or member.

`<example>`

```
<example>...</example>
```

Denotes an example (used by documentation generators). This usually contains both description text and source code (source code is typically within a `<c>` or `<code>` tags).

`<c>`

```
<c>...</c>
```

Indicates an inline code snippet. This tag is usually used inside an `<example>` block.

`<code>`

```
<code>...</code>
```

Indicates a multiline code sample. This tag is usually used inside an `<example>` block.

`<see>`

```
<see cref="member">...</see>
```

Inserts an inline cross-reference to another type or member. HTML documentation generators typically convert this to a hyperlink. The compiler emits a warning if the type or member name is invalid.

`<seealso>`

```
<seealso cref="member">...</seealso>
```

Cross references another type or member. Documentation generators typically write this into a separate "See Also" section at the bottom of the page.

`<paramref>`

```
<paramref name="name"/>
```

References a parameter from within a `<summary>` or `<remarks>` tag.

`<list>`

```
<list type=[ bullet | number | table ]>
  <listheader>
    <term>...</term>
    <description>...</description>
  </listheader>
  <item>
    <term>...</term>
    <description>...</description>
  </item>
</list>
```

Instructs documentation generators to emit a bulleted, numbered, or table-style list.

ara>
    <para>...</para>

Instructs documentation generators to format the contents into a separate paragraph.

`<include>`

Merges an external XML file that contains documentation. The path attribute denotes an XPath query to a specific element in that file.

Framework Overview

Almost all the capabilities of the .NET Framework are exposed via a vast set of managed types. These types are organized into hierarchical namespaces and packaged into a set of assemblies, which together with the CLR comprise the .NET platform.

Some of the .NET types are used directly by the CLR and are essential for the managed hosting environment. These types reside in an assembly called *mscorlib.dll* and include C#'s built-in types, as well as the basic collection classes, and types for stream processing, serialization, reflection, threading, and native interoperability.

At a level above this are additional types that "flesh out" the CLR-level functionality, providing features such as XML, networking, and LINQ. These reside in *System.dll*, *System. Xml.dll*, and *System.Core.dll* (new to Framework 3.5) and, together with *mscorlib*, they provide a rich programming environment upon which the rest of the Framework is built.

The remainder of the .NET Framework consists of applied APIs, most of which cover three areas of functionality:

- User interface technologies
- Backend technologies
- Distributed system technologies

Table 16 shows the history of compatibility between each version of C#, CLR, and the .NET Framework. Interestingly, C# 3.0 targets a new Framework version while using the same CLR version as its predecessor. To be precise, C# 3.0 targets an *updated* version of CLR 2.0, which is installed as part of Framework 3.5. This update is designed not to break compatibility with existing applications.

Table 16. C#, CLR, and .NET Framework versions

C# version	CLR version	Framework versions
1.0	1.0	1.0
1.1	1.1	1.1
2.0	2.0	2.0
		3.0
3.0	2.0 (updated)	3.5

The Core Framework

System types

The most fundamental types live directly in the System namespace. These include C#'s built-in types, the Exception base class, the Enum, and Array, and Delegate base classes, Nullable and Type. The System namespace also includes:

- DateTime for representing a date and optional time
- DateTimeOffset for representing a DateTime + UTC offset (new to Framework 3.5)
- TimeSpan for representing a duration of time
- Guid for representing a globally unique identifier
- Math (static) for performing mathematical functions
- Random for generating random numbers
- Convert and BitConverter for converting between various types

he System namespace also defines standard interfaces such as IDisposable, IFormattable, and IComparable (the latter provides a standard protocol for order comparison).

Text processing

The System.Text namespace contains the StringBuilder class (the editable or *mutable* cousin of string), and the types for working with text encodings, such as UTF-8 (Encoding and its subtypes).

System.Text.RegularExpressions contains the Regex class and supporting types to perform advanced pattern-based search and replace operations. The samples in LINQPad (*www. linqpad.net*) include a section demonstrating the use of regular expressions.

Collections

The .NET Framework offers a variety of classes for managing collections of items. These include both list-based structures such as List<> (think *variable-length array*), and Stack<> and LinkedList<>—as well as dictionary-based structures such as Dictionary<,> (a hashtable) and SortedDictionary<> (a red-black tree). The classes work in conjunction with a set of standard interfaces that unify their common characteristics, namely, IEnumerable<>, ICollection<>, IList<>, and IDictionary<,>. All collection types are defined in the following namespaces:

```
System.Collections              // Nongeneric collections
System.Collections.Generic      // Generic collections
System.Collections.Specialized
System.Collections.ObjectModel  // Bases for custom types
```

NOTE

C# 3.0 in a Nutshell covers the core framework in detail in Chapters 5–24.

Queries

The types for writing local LINQ queries (as covered in the book) reside in the System.Linq namespace (in the *System.Core.dll* assembly). The Framework also provides APIs for writing LINQ queries over SQL tables (LINQ to SQL) and in-memory XML documents:

```
System.Linq              // Basic infrastructure
System.Xml.Linq          // LINQ to XML
System.Data.Linq         // LINQ to SQL
System.Linq.Expressions  // For building expressions
```

You can find examples on using LINQ to XML and LINQ to XML in LINQPad at *www.linqpad.net*.

XML

XML is used widely within the .NET Framework and thus is supported extensively. LINQ to XML includes a lightweight XML document object model that can be constructed and queried through LINQ. The Framework also provides an older "clunky" W3C-compliant DOM (XmlDocument) and classes to support XML schemas, stylesheets, and XPath. Finally, there's XmlReader and XmlWriter, which are performant low-level forward-only XML reader/writers. The XML namespaces are:

```
System.Xml           // XmlReader, XmlWriter + old W3C DOM
System.Xml.Linq      // The LINQ to XML DOM
System.Xml.Schema    // Support for XSD
System.Xml.XPath     // XPath query language
System.Xml.Xsl       // Stylesheet support
```

The easiest XML DOM to work with is LINQ to XML (this is true even if you don't use the LINQ operators). The LINQ to XML API makes the W3C-compliant API largely redundant, as well as reducing the need to use XPath and XSL.

The Framework also includes an attribute-driven XML serialization engine in System.Xml.Serialization.

The Framework provides a stream-based model for low-level input/output. Streams are typically used to read and write directly to files and network connections, and they can be chained or wrapped in decorator streams to add compression or encryption functionality. The System.IO namespace contains the low-level stream types (starting with the abstract Stream type), and types for working with files and directories (File, FileInfo, Directory, DirectoryInfo, DriveInfo, and Path), as well as isolated storage:

```
System.IO                  // File support + stream types
System.IO.Pipes            // Support for Windows pipes
System.IO.Compression      // Compression streams
System.IO.IsolatedStorage  // Isolated storage streams
```

Networking

You can directly access low-level network protocols such as HTTP, FTP, TCP/IP, and SMTP via the types in System.Net:

```
System.Net
System.Net.Mail        // For sending mail via SMTP
System.Net.Sockets     // TCP, UDP, and IP
```

The WebClient class is a wrapper that encapsulates most of the client-side functionality for communicating via HTTP and FTP. The Socket class provides raw access to TCP and UDP.

Serialization

The Framework provides a number of systems for saving and restoring objects to a binary or text representation. Such systems are required for distributed application technologies, such as Windows Communication Foundation (WCF), Web Services, and Remoting, and also to save and restore objects to a file. In total, there are three serialization engines:

Data contract serializion engine (FW 3.5)
    The most modern engine, used implicitly by WCF. This engine is excellent at interoperable messaging and for serializing to XML files (particularly when version

tolerance or the need to preserve shared object re̶~~ences~~ is important). It can serialize to either XML binary.

Binary serialization engine
This engine is powerful, easy to use, and well supported throughout the .NET Framework. Remoting uses binary serialization—including when communicating between two application domains in the same process. The disadvantage of this engine is that it tightly couples a type's internal structure to the format of the serialized data, resulting in poor version tolerance. Further, it cannot serialize to simple XML files.

XML serialization engine
This engine produces *only* XML files and is less powerful than other engines in saving and restoring a complex object graph (it cannot restore shared object references). It's the most flexible of the three, however, in following an arbitrary XML structure. ASMX Web Services implicitly uses the XML serialization engine (Web Services implemented through WCF, however, uses the data contract engine).

The types that support the data contact and binary engines live in `System.Runtime.Serialization`. The attribute-driven XML serialization engine lives in `System.Xml.Serialization`.

Assemblies, reflection, and attributes

The assemblies into which C# programs compile comprise executable instructions (stored as intermediate language or IL) and metadata, which describes the program's types, members, and attributes. Through reflection, you can inspect this metadata at runtime, and do such things as retrieve attribute information, inspect types and members, and dynamically invoke methods. With `Reflection.Emit`, you can construct new code on the fly.

...e types for reflection reside the following namespaces:

```
System
System.Reflection
System.Reflection.Emit
```

The window to most of the reflection data is a class called Type; you can obtain an instance via C#'s typeof operator or by calling GetType( ) on an object instance. The window to most assembly-related data is the Assembly type.

Security

The .NET Framework provides its own permission-based security layer, comprising code access security and role-based security. Code access security allows you to both sandbox other assemblies and be sandboxed yourself (limiting the kinds of operations that can be performed). The central type for enforcing permission-based security is IPermission.

```
System.Security
System.Security.Permissions
System.Security.Policy
```

The Framework also provides types for encryption (symmetric and public-key), hashing, and data protection in the System.Security.Cryptography namespace.

Threading

Multithreading allows you to execute code in parallel. Central to multithreading is the Thread class and synchronization constructs such as exclusive locking (supported by C#'s lock statement). A free and extensive article on multithreading is available online at *www.albahari.com/threading*.

All types for threading are in the System.Threading namespace.

Application domains

The CLR provides an additional level of isolation within a process called an *application domain*. A .NET process normally runs in a single automatically created application domain. Creating additional application domains in the same process is useful for such purposes as unit testing. AppDomain type is defined in the System namespace, and encapsulates access to application domains.

Native interoperability

You can interoperate with native and Win32 code through the P/Invoke system. The .NET runtime allows you to call native functions, register callbacks, map data structures, and interoperate with native and COM data types. The namespace providing this support is System.Runtime. InteropServices.

Diagnostics

The Framework provides logging and assertion facilities through the Debug, Trace, and TraceListener classes in System.Diagnostics. Also in this namespace is the Process class for interacting with other processes, classes for writing to the Windows event log, and types for reading/writing performance counters for monitoring.

User Interface Technologies

The .NET Framework provides three APIs for user-interface-based applications:

ASP.NET (System.Web.UI)
> For writing thin-client applications that run over a standard web browser

Windows Presentation Foundation (System.Windows)
> For writing rich-client applications that target the .NET Framework 3.0

Windows Forms (System.Windows.Forms)
> For writing rich-client applications that target the classic Windows API, supported in all versions of the .NET Framework

general, a thin-client application amounts to a web site; a rich-client application is a program the end user must download or install on the client computer.

ASP.NET

Applications written using ASP.NET host under Windows IIS and can be accessed from almost any web browser. Here are its advantages over rich-client technologies:

- Zero deployment at the client end
- Clients can run a non-Windows platform
- Updates are easily deployed

Further, because most of what you write in an ASP.NET application runs on the server, you design your data access layer to run in the same application domain—without limiting security or scalability. In contrast, a rich client that does the same is not generally as secure or scalable. (The solution, with the rich client, is to insert a *middle tier* between the client and database. The middle tier runs on a remote application server [often alongside the database server] and communicates with the rich clients via WCF, Web Services, or Remoting.)

Another benefit of ASP.NET is that it's mature—it was introduced with the first version of .NET and has been refined with each subsequent .NET release.

The limitations of ASP.NET are largely a reflection of the limitations of thin-client systems in general:

- A web browser interface significantly restricts what you can do.
- Maintaining state on the client—or on behalf of the client—is cumbersome.

You can improve the interactivity and responsiveness, however, through client-side scripting or technologies such as AJAX; see *http://ajax.asp.net/*.

The types for writing ASP.NET applications are in System.Web.UI namespace and its subnamespaces, and th are packed in the *System.Web.dll* assembly.

Windows Presentation Foundation

WPF is a rich-client technology new to Framework 3.0. Framework 3.0 comes installed on Windows Vista—and is available as a separate download for Windows XP SP2. Here are its benefits:

- It supports sophisticated graphics, such as arbitrary transformations, 3D rendering, and true transparency.

- Its primary measurement unit is not pixel-based, so applications display correctly at any DPI (dots per inch).

- It has extensive dynamic layout support, which means you can localize an application without danger of elements overlapping.

- Rendering uses DirectX and is fast, taking good advantage of graphics hardware acceleration.

- User interfaces can be described declaratively in XAML files that can be maintained independently of the "code-behind" files—this helps to separate appearance from functionality.

Here are its limitations:

- The technology is less mature than Windows Forms or ASP.NET.

- Its size and complexity make for a steep learning curve.

- Your clients must run Windows Vista—or Windows XP with Framework 3.0 or later.

The types for writing WPF applications are in the System. Windows namespace and all subnamespaces except for System. Windows.Forms.

Windows Forms is a rich-client API that—like ASP.NET—is as old as the .NET Framework. Compared to WPF, Windows Forms is a relatively simple technology that provides most of the features you need in writing a typical Windows application. It also has significant relevancy in maintaining legacy applications. It has a number of drawbacks, though, compared to WPF:

- Controls are positioned and sized in pixels, making it easy to write applications that break on clients whose DPI settings differ from the developer's.

- The API for drawing nonstandard controls is GDI+, which—although reasonably flexible—is slow in rendering large areas (and without double buffering, it flickers horribly).

- Controls lack true transparency.

- Dynamic layout is difficult to get right reliably.

The last point is an excellent reason to favor WPF over Windows Forms—even if you're writing a business application that needs just a user interface and not a "user experience." The layout elements in WPF, such as `Grid`, make it easy to assemble labels and text boxes such that they always align—even after language changing localization—without messy logic and without any flickering. Further, you don't have to bow to the lowest common denominator in screen resolution—WPF layout elements have been designed from the outset to adapt properly to resizing.

On the positive side, Windows Forms is relatively simple to learn and has a wealth of support in third-party controls.

The Windows Forms types are in the `System.Windows.Forms` (in *System.Windows.Forms.dll*) and `System.Drawing` (in *System.Drawing.dll*) namespaces. The latter also contains the GDI+ types for drawing custom controls.

Backend Technologies

ADO.NET

ADO.NET is the managed data access API. Although the
name is derived from ADO (ActiveX Data Objects), the technology is completely different. ADO.NET comprises two
major components:

Provider layer
> The provider model defines common classes and inter-
> faces for low-level access to database providers. These
> interfaces comprise connections, commands, adapters,
> and readers (forward-only, read-only cursors over a data-
> base). The Framework ships with native support for
> Microsoft SQL Server and Oracle, and it has OLE-DB
> and ODBC providers.

DataSet model
> A DataSet is a structured cache of data. It resembles a
> primitive in-memory database, which defines SQL con-
> structs such as tables, rows, columns, relationships, con-
> straints, and views. By programming against a cache of
> data, you can reduce the number of trips to the server,
> increasing server scalability and the responsiveness of a
> rich-client user interface. DataSets are serializable and
> designed to be sent across the wire between client and
> server applications.

LINQ to SQL sits above the provider layer, leveraging the
lower-level connection and reader types. With LINQ to SQL,
you avoid having to manually construct and parameterize SQL
statements, reducing the volume of code in an application's
data access layer and improving its type safety. LINQ to SQL
also partially avoids the need for DataSets through its object-
relational mapping system. DataSets have some advantages,

ough, such as being able to serialize state changes to XML (something particularly useful in multitier applications). LINQ and DataSets can interoperate, however; for instance, you can use LINQ to perform type-safe queries over DataSet objects.

Windows Workflow

Windows Workflow is a framework for modeling and managing potentially long-running business processes. It targets a standard runtime library, providing consistency and interoperability. Workflow also helps reduce coding for dynamically controlled decision-making trees.

It is not strictly a backend technology—you can use it anywhere (an example is page flow in the UI).

Workflow is another part of the shipment of assemblies that came with the .NET Framework 3.0, so like WPF, it leverages services that require the operating system support of Windows Vista—or Windows XP after a Framework 3.0 installation. The Workflow types are defined in (and are below) the System.WorkFlow namespace.

COM+ and MSMQ

The Framework allows you to interoperate with COM+ for services such as distributed transactions, via types in the System.EnterpriseServices namespace. It also supports MSMQ (Microsoft Message Queuing) for asynchronous, one-way messaging through types in System.Messaging.

Distributed System Technologies

Windows Communication Foundation

WCF is the communications infrastructure new to Framework 3.0. WCF is flexible and configurable enough to make both of its predecessors—Remoting and (ASMX) Web Services—*mostly* redundant.

WCF, Remoting, and Web Services are all alike in that t.
implement the following basic model in allowing a client an
server application to communicate:

- On the server, you indicate what methods you'd like
  remote client applications to be able to call.
- On the client, you specify or infer the *signatures* of the
  server methods you'd like to call.
- On both the server and the client, you choose a transport and communication protocol (in WCF, this is done
  through a *binding*).
- The client establishes a connection to the server.
- The client calls a remote method, which executes trans-
  parently on the server.

WCF further decouples the client and server through service
contracts and data contracts. Conceptually, the client sends an
(XML) message to an endpoint on a remote *service*, rather
than directly invoking a remote method. One of the benefits of
this decoupling: clients have no dependency on the .NET platform or on any proprietary communication protocols.

WCF is highly configurable and provides the most extensive
support for standardized messaging protocols, including WS-*.
This lets you communicate with parties running different software—possibly on different platforms—while still supporting
advanced features such as encryption. Another benefit of WCF
is that you can change protocols without needing to change
other aspects of your client or server applications.

The types for communicating with WCF are in, and under,
the `System.ServiceModel` namespace.

Remoting and (ASMX) Web Services

Remoting and ASMX Web Services are WCF's predecessors
and are almost redundant in WCF's wake—although Remoting still has a niche in communicating between application
domains within the same process.

.moting's functionality is geared toward tightly coupled applications. A typical example is when the client and server are both .NET applications written by the same company (or companies sharing common assemblies). Communication typically involves exchanging potentially complex custom .NET objects that the Remoting infrastructure serializes and deserializes without needing intervention.

The functionality of ASMX Web Services is geared toward loosely coupled or SOA-style applications. A typical example is a server designed to accept simple SOAP-based messages that originate from clients running a variety of software—on a variety of platforms. Web Services can only use HTTP and SOAP as transport and formatting protocols and applications are normally hosted under IIS. The benefits of interoperability come at a performance cost—a Web Services application is typically slower, in both execution and development time, than a well-designed Remoting application.

The types for Remoting are in or under `System.Runtime.Remoting`; the types for Web Services are under `System.Web.Services`.

CardSpace

CardSpace comprises the final new piece of the .NET 3.0 shipment. It is a token-based authentication and identity management protocol designed to simplify password management for end users. CardSpace builds on open XML standards, and parties can participate independently of Microsoft.

With CardSpace, a user can hold multiple identities, which are maintained by a third party (the *identity provider*). When a user wants to access a resource at site X, the user authenticates to the identity provider, which then issues a token to site X. This avoids having to provide a password directly to site X, and it reduces the number of identities that the user needs to maintain.

WCF allows you to specify a CardSpace identity when connecting through a secure HTTP channel through types in the `System.IdentityModel.Claims` and `System.IdentityModel.Policy` namespaces.

Index

Symbols

& (ampersand)
  address-of pointer
      operator, 188
  bitwise-and operator, 27, 32
  && conditional and
      operator, 31
* (asterisk)
  dereference pointer
      operator, 188
  multiplication operator, 25
@ (at sign)
  prefixing identifiers, 9
\ (backslash)
  escape sequence for, 33, 34
  preceding escape
      sequences, 32
{} (braces)
  enclosing statement
      blocks, 10, 58
^ (caret)
  exclusive-or operator, 27
: (colon)
  terminating label
      statement, 64
" (double quote)
  enclosing string literals, 33
  escape sequence for, 32

= (equal sign)
  == equality operator, 30, 150
  => in lambda
      expressions, 129
! (exclamation point)
  not operator, 31
  != inequality operator, 30,
      150
/ (forward slash)
  division operator, 25
  // preceding comments, 11
  /// documentation
      comment, 195
  /* ... */ enclosing multi-line
      comments, 11
  /** ... */ documentation
      comment, 195
< (left angle bracket)
  less than operator, 150
  <= less than or equal
      operator, 150
  << shift left operator, 27
- (minus sign)
  subtraction operator, 25
  -- decrement operator, 25
  -> pointer-to-member
      operator, 188, 190
  -= removing delegate
      operands, 119

We'd like to hear your suggestions for improving our indexes. Send email to
index@oreilly.com.

lifted, for nullable types, 149
list of, 52–55
logical operators, 54
overloading, 152–156
pointer operators, 188
precedence of, 51, 52–55
query operators, LINQ, 160, 166–169
relational operators, 54, 150
ternary operators, 50
unary operators, 50, 53
or operator, bitwise (|), 27, 32
or operator, conditional (||), 31
OrderBy operator, LINQ, 167, 180
OrderByDescending operator, LINQ, 167, 180
ordering operators, LINQ, 166, 167
out argument, 47
outer variables, in lambda expressions, 132
overflow check operators, 26
OverflowException class, 26
overflows on integral types, 26
overloading constructors, 71
overloading methods, 70, 90
overloading operators, 152–156
override modifier, 85

P

PadLeft method, strings, 35
PadRight method, strings, 35
<para> XML tag, 198
<param> XML tag, 196
parameterless constructor constraint, 114
parameterless constructors, 72, 89
parameters of attributes, 184
parameters of methods, 45–48, 71
  any number of, allowing, 48

generic, 111, 113–114
multiple return values with, 47
<paramref> XML tag, 197
params modifier, 48
partial classes, 80
partial methods, 81
Pascal case, 8
passing arguments by reference, 46, 47, 71
passing arguments by value, 45, 71
percent sign (%)
  remainder operator, 25
<permission> XML tag, 196
pinning objects, 189
plug-in methods, 118
plus sign (+)
  addition operator, 25
  concatenation operator, 34
  += combining delegates, 119
  ++ increment operator, 25
pointer operators, 188
pointers, 187–192
pointer-to-member operator (->), 188, 190
polymorphism, 83
positional parameters of attributes, 185
positive infinity value, 28
#pragma warning directive, 194
precedence of operators, 51
predefined types, 11, 13, 20
preprocessor directives, 192–195
primary expressions, 50
primitive types, 14, 21
private access modifier, 76, 97
projection operators, LINQ, 166, 167
properties, 74–76
protected access modifier, 97
protected internal access modifier, 97